371. 904435   SIN

KU-504-733

1859307

Access to ICT

Other titles in the series:

Access to History
Curriculum Planning and Practical Activities for Pupils with Learning Difficulties
Andrew Turner
£15.00
1-85346-857-6

Access to Science
Curriculum Planning and Practical Activities for Pupils with Learning Difficulties
Claire Marvin and Chris Stokoe
£14.00
1-85346-917-3

Access to Citizenship
Curriculum Planning and Practical Activities for Pupils with Learning Difficulties
Ann Fergusson and Hazel Lawson
£14.00
1-85346-910-6

Access to ICT

**Curriculum planning and practical activities
for pupils with learning difficulties**

UNIVERSITY OF WALES COLLEGE NEWPORT
LIBRARY AND INFORMATION SERVICES CAERLEON

Liz Flavell, Liz Singleton and Iain Ross

David Fulton Publishers

David Fulton Publishers Ltd
The Chiswick Centre, 414 Chiswick High Road, London W4 5TF

www.fultonpublishers.co.uk

First published in Great Britain in 2004 by David Fulton Publishers
10 9 8 7 6 5 4 3 2 1

David Fulton Publishers is a division of Granada Learning Limited, part of ITV plc.

Note: The right of Liz Flavell, Liz Singleton and Iain Ross to be identified as the authors of this work has been asserted by them in accordance with the Copyright, Designs and Patents Act 1988.

Copyright © Liz Flavell, Liz Singleton and Iain Ross 2004

British Library Cataloguing in Publication Data
A catalogue record for this book is available from the British Library.

ISBN 1–84312–089–5

All rights reserved. No part of this publication may be reproduced, stored in a retrieval system or transmitted, in any form, or by any means, electronic, mechanical, photocopying, recording or otherwise, without the prior permission of the publishers.

Typeset by FiSH Books, London
Printed and bound in Great Britain

Contents

Augmentative switches

Communication

Control

Enjoyable experiences

Supportive environment

Success

Introduction

Inclusion is high on the national agenda. As part of the inclusion initiative in Leeds, a project was launched to review enhancing provision for pupils with special educational needs in our special schools and to seek and develop opportunities for access to education alongside mainstream peers.

> In Leeds, our policy for inclusion is underpinned by the key principles of access to high quality schooling for all, in their neighbourhood schools. It is an integral part of our overall raising achievement agenda which aims to ensure that all pupils, including those with special educational needs, have access to the highest quality education. (Education Leeds 2000)

It became clear that staff from mainstream and special schools would need to share expertise in order to develop new styles of teaching and deeper understanding of the subject pedagogy. This was ambitious and aimed at challenging fundamental beliefs and attitudes to learning and achievement.

Two inclusion specialists, Liz Flavell and June Wilson, set out to raise the profile of pupil achievements with mainstream colleagues. Thought was given to the focus key stage, and the subjects for initial pilot.

As the differences in attitude to attainment appear to be stark, when students embark upon GCSE studies, this seemed a good place to start. It immediately raised questions, which we hoped we could answer. The subject had to be practical, involve a range of sensory experiences and promote key skill development. It had to be Food Technology, as we already had contacts in mainstream schools in that area who were willing to establish collaborative networks between special and mainstream schools. Looking at the units of study in terms of texture, taste, smell, feel and visual appeal was enough to set the team off working on the GCSE units.

The team was driven by enthusiasm, commitment and a vision of the end product that could be used by schools across the board.

Using the skills and knowledge of the team members, a Key Stage 4 scheme of work has been written, incorporating learning objectives, outcomes and expectations linked to Performance Descriptors ('P' scales), National Curriculum levels and the GCSE syllabus. A single planning document could not cover the range of needs not served by the GCSE syllabus, so the scheme became a road with three lanes converging at the same point – a common accreditation certificate. Red lane, 'P' 1-4; Blue, 'P' 4–8; and Green, 'P' 7; to Level 1 NC. Each lane is broadly related to targets for attainment, though staff and students are encouraged to be adventurous, swapping lanes occasionally to make that journey as challenging – but attainable – as possible for each individual.

Other subjects have been tackled including textiles and art, and all have been funded by Education Leeds who seconded the teachers out of school to set up appropriately staffed working parties.

However, when the City Learning Centres were being built in Leeds, anxious to be part of the latest technological initiative and backed by the visionary head teacher at Penny Field, we set out to harness all the things the CLCs had to offer our pupils.

When one is struck by what seems like a good idea, and meets others who have similar ideas, a creative force comes into being. The three authors of this book devised, implemented, delivered, evaluated and disseminated the programme described herein together.

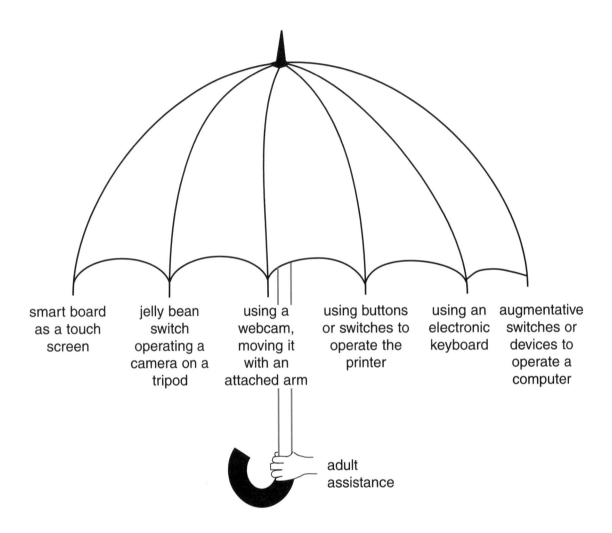

smart board as a touch screen

jelly bean switch operating a camera on a tripod

using a webcam, moving it with an attached arm

using buttons or switches to operate the printer

using an electronic keyboard

augmentative switches or devices to operate a computer

adult assistance

Figure A Pulling together an ICT-based activity in an inclusive environment

Liz Singleton and Iain Ross had worked together in the City Learning Centre from its inception. Liz had the vision for the strategic development of the centre for all the community, and Iain shared her skills of making them accessible to all, including gifted and talented, the hard to teach, those with learning difficulties, mainstream examination groups and members of the local community who wanted to access the technology.

Liz Flavell came along in her role as inclusion teacher for pupils with profound and multiple learning difficulties, eager to ensure that the City Learning Centre would be accessible to the pupils. The three professionals, coming from different areas of expertise, immediately saw the possibilities of working together to develop a versatile programme using the very latest technology for the benefit of pupils with complex needs.

The nature of the programme is such that it enthuses all who have the opportunity to use it with pupils and to develop areas to cover their own needs. Seeing the pupils benefit so much from this learning environment and experience is part of the reward teachers and others gain for getting involved in this process of helping pupils with a range of complex needs to access ICT.

By involving different groups of staff in the programme there was more 'know-how' available to adapt teaching styles and resources to involve and promote attainment of their included students. Most importantly, the pupils made progress by accepting challenges and attaining or exceeding the ambitious targets we set them. Parents and carers could not be said just to value the recognition of their child's achievement. Some even cried with pride.

The key to good inclusive practice, as these experiences have shown time and again, is to develop working parties of teachers and others to share experiences and expertise, whether it be of special needs or subject, and all are required to make the inclusive experience as good as it can get.

CHAPTER ONE

Principles and process of inclusion

All LEAs work within the same national legislative framework and the disturbing variations between LEAs across England leave significant cause for concern. The variations between LEAs add weight to the argument that more should be done by central and local government to unify the approach of all LEAs to the law and DfES guidance covering the education of disabled children. Put simply, is it fair to pupils and their families – and others – that in 2001, a disabled pupil in Lambeth was more than 6 times as likely to be segregated in a special school than a pupil in Newham, just ten miles away? (Norwich 2002:25)

This plea for national direction to be given to LEAs to create a fairer and more equitable system of inclusion would necessarily run alongside the 'bottom-up' approach of pockets of good or excellent practice for pupils included in the full range of educational provision in some areas of the country.

Within the underlying frustration in this concluding section of a CSIE document, *LEA Inclusion Trends in England 1997–2001*, is the suggestion that inclusion should be imposed in some way on LEAs and then, necessarily, onto schools. Without the schools developing an ethos of celebrating difference reflected in development planning and preparation and delivery of the curriculum, the imposition of inclusion would surely create more resentment and attitudinal problems than if an almost organic growth within establishments were allowed with the willingness, energy and imagination to embrace all pupils within their community. The process of inclusion does not stop in establishments where acceptance of difference is expected from all staff, including the caretaker, the lunchtime supervisors and any voluntary organisations that have an input. The governors need to be embracing the necessary physical, social and curriculum changes to include the needs of all pupils, while the senior management act as enablers for the rest of the school staff.

Historical overview within the present day context

The historical perspective of inclusion is a review of the issues that frame the development of education for pupils with special educational needs. The latest changes to learning alongside mainstream peers, as all pupils access a high-quality education, do not just mean that a minority of the pupils are accommodated in the lesson with the appropriate challenges based on the national requirements of the curriculum content set for the majority; it is also about curriculum access for all, with suitably designed planning that accommodates all the pupils' requirements.

The progress towards inclusive education is fraught with outdated terminology and a system with disability and difference acquiring a marginalised place in education and thus the wider society beyond:

The sociology and politics of special education have uncovered ways in which the vested interests in the education system and beyond have conspired to subvert any progress towards more liberal practices and forms of provision. (Dyson 2001: 2)

Since 1972, when pupils with the most complex needs have been deemed 'educable', the education system has had a place of its own creation for these pupils. Part of the special school system has been given to pupils who were labelled mentally handicapped or in need of special care. Trainee teachers were on special courses which qualified them as 'teachers of the mentally handicapped'. The specialist nature of the course content would mean that much of the training was undertaken separately from the 'normal' teachers. All the systems were in place to extend the difference of pupils with learning difficulties from their peers. That they were educators now, rather than trainers, seemed to emphasise the differences rather than look at common aims for all pupils. By educating teachers separately, it ensured that the special needs of the pupils were seen to need different skills and an alternative professional workforce. To some extent, this provided a body of professionals, including teachers, who had a vested interest in maintaining and strengthening a *status quo* of separate provision. Over the next 20 years, special schools were built away from the mainstream provision, staffed by teachers who had undergone separate training and support assistants who may have previously worked with the pupils in the pre-education days when they were the responsibility of social services and health authorities. The innovation of using a variety of methods to address the pupils' difficulties also emphasised their differences, rather than a commonality with the majority of learners.

This brings us to the Warnock Report and the 1981 Education Act, which allowed more pupils with learning difficulties into mainstream provision with additional support. This introduced the system of Statements of Special Educational Need, which allocated pupils to a suitable school and provided the extra resources necessary for individual pupils. This still left a proportion of the population being educated in special schools, providing a specialist curriculum and resources.

The integration agenda took increasing numbers of individual pupils within the range of complex learning difficulties into mainstream, supported by funding generated by the needs addressed on the Statement. So a smaller population with a wide range of needs was left within the special school sector, often supported by specialist educational, health and social services staff. This has perpetuated the medical model of viewing the needs of pupils rather than the educational or social model. Indeed, Statements of Special Educational Need will still identify the more common syndromes as an explanation of the child's special educational need. For example, some characteristics associated with Down's Syndrome are significant for the allocation of school provision, but differences among the Down's population show that levels of need vary enormously among the population. It gives very little information about educational need, although it uses a medical term as a descriptor of the child.

As Kenn Jupp says, 'Since people who have Down's Syndrome vary from each other as much as people who have driving licences do, this tells us nothing about his/her special needs' (Jupp 1992: 28).

The days of schools designated for the delicate (frequently pupils with asthma, disfigurements or other purely medical needs) are gone. Instead we have a process of Statements that still relies frequently on medical evidence of learning needs. Anecdotally, this has even included pupils with diabetes, a complaint not associated with any learning or access difficulty. Physical problems leading to access issues are, of course, necessary identifiers of some needs for specialist equipment for curriculum access, but again the current system leads to an over-resourcing of facilities for some needs in terms of finance, while other difficulties are overlooked in terms of curriculum access. To equip a school with lifts, ramps and widened doorways suitable for independent wheelchair users makes the building into a community facility. What it does not do is make it an inclusive school or centre. In order to access many areas of the curriculum across academic, practical and social requirements, the fittings in the building need some adapted parts in order for the pupils to be fully included. It also requires a funding allocation to train staff in using equipment readily available with some flexibility in order for the priority to be that all the pupils follow the same broad curriculum. The inclusion statement in the National Curriculum 2000 emphasises that the majority of special needs can be accommodated within the differentiation of lessons that all teachers will necessarily do. This will not have a detrimental effect on other pupils, but will broaden the delivery of the subject to benefit all pupils. Lack of awareness or lack of training and communication about the needs of pupils with special needs or disabilities includes:

1. No inclusive PE for wheelchair users. The challenge this provides for PE teachers is also within the remit of the National Curriculum statement. Support by a physiotherapist as well as training in handling techniques and specialist hoists or other equipment may appear daunting to the PE co-ordinator, but advice and help may be available if planning time for professionals to work together is used imaginatively. Often therapists see the SENCO or the school assistants supporting the individual. How much better it would be if the health and education workers could get together and share skills to optimise the education of pupils with special needs?

2. No access to technology rooms due to the positioning of workbenches. Within mainstream schools, even those built with physical access, room layouts have not included the extra space necessary for the wheelchair user. Even more space is needed if the pupil can manoeuvre a chair independently.

3. No access to resistant materials lessons, on health and safety grounds. By looking at the curriculum content, there can be provision for pupils to access some materials that do not require delicate fine motor control, or a pupil can work under the direction of a peer partner. This is not a way of working that would be limited to those with special needs, but has proved to be beneficial to many other pupils.

4. Limited access to the dining-hall where the design is such that the tables and stools are attached, with lack of wheelchair space except at the end of tables. Peer has to collect dinner, as the canteen-style service area is not wide enough for wheelchairs or supportive seating.

5. Limited alternative switches in the computer suite. Specialist help is needed in order to provide the range of switches and access equipment in order to make information technology accessible to all pupils.

6. One-to-one support for pupils throughout the day is used without flexibility and imagination. The constant presence of an adult then leads to limited opportunities for interaction with peers.

7. Limited support from the health services – speech therapists, occupational therapists and physiotherapists. The individual nature of the caseloads means that they tend to be assigned to individual pupils within the school population. This creates a division in the provision of necessary services to pupils, rather than encouraging interaction and flexible working practices, allowing professionals to work together and devise collaborative lessons whereby the other pupils receive the same high-quality

education. A more flexible remit means that those with special needs are provided for within the same planning and delivery.

8. Limited access to specialist teachers in special schools who could advise on a consultative basis.

9. Lack of areas for pupil dignity, such as hygiene suites, and lack of adequate hoists for use in curriculum areas, such as drama and PE, and for necessary changes of position during the day.

This list is born of the frustration felt by working in schools in both phases with pupils who are statemented as having special educational needs and where these needs are not met, not from lack of willingness by staff, but often from a lack of specialist support.

Tensions and Resolution

A mainstream high school has recently admitted a small number of pupils with mobility difficulties into the school. ACCESS funding has been granted for purchasing rise and fall electrical equipment in technology while the pupils have no rise and fall tables in other curricular areas, using trays on their chairs. This prevents working alongside their peers to some extent in the majority of 'academic' subject areas.

That isolation is increased by poorly thought-out equipment for the settings the pupils are taught in is largely overlooked by schools and others. This can be easily overcome by more thought being put into the social aspects of the learning environment. To share tables, facilitating the sharing of ideas and joint problem-solving with one's peers, is so important at any age or stage of a school career.

In another school, a pupil who has problems with fine motor skills as well as mobility difficulties has no access to a laptop computer to assist her in her work. Consequently, the pupil herself feels that she is falling behind due to her poor and laborious handwriting. She is very vocal in her desire to work with a laptop and is highly computer-literate (her hobbies include designing websites), yet she struggles with handwriting which is leaving her behind her classmates in work. While agreeing that the mechanics of writing and fine motor skills are important, a more proactive approach is needed.

An overview of the necessary equipment needs of the pupils and a more equitable use of funding, with decisions on use of available resources made by a group of professionals and the parents looking at the long-term future of pupils with augmentative equipment needs, is needed.

The tensions between the needs of the pupils and the perceived need of the school to fulfil their obligation to pupils with specific disabilities can be resolved with more informed choice or with more shared experience and expertise available to those charged with making the curriculum accessible for the pupils. Ideally, curriculum and peer access would be considered along with the physical access when new inclusive schools are designed. Equally, the design of dining areas, common rooms and sixth-form blocks needs to look at all the needs of the pupils. Curriculum and social access seems to be secondary to physical access when the original plans are drawn up. Surely these should go in tandem, rather than being left to the yearly planning of the school's overstretched SENCO.

Current principles and practice

The new Code of Practice and the SEN and Disability Act 2001 are changing the face of education of pupils with a range of disabilities and are encouraging schools and teachers to view each other in terms of educators of all pupils. Indeed, the Code of Practice states that 'every teacher is a teacher of special needs' (DfES 2001a: 38). This phrase has far-reaching implications for both special and mainstream schools to broaden their thinking. It is no longer the preserve of the pupils to 'fit' as best they can into a culture and community that is fixed in its practice, inflexible in the daily practice of including special needs into the classroom or working individually with a statemented pupil away from the rest of the class for large chunks of the school day.

> An inclusive ethos implies that all children should be educated together for curricular and social reasons. There is little evidence that withdrawing them for particular periods is beneficial. (Thomas *et al.* 1997: 193)

It is this access to the curriculum in a meaningful fashion that is vital in order for inclusion to gain the credibility it deserves as a principle with the strategic policy-makers at local and national level and with the practitioners in classrooms across all age phases. '[Government] cannot legislate ethos; neither can it, if one is being realistic, do much to influence school culture from the outside' (Ibid.: 194).

The tensions present within the school system created by league tables, SATs and academic excellence are in themselves anti-inclusive. The pupils with Statements of Special Educational Need can be exempt from these results, but the drive to lower the number of statements leaves some pupils vulnerable to pressure from within certain schools to attend a more accommodating and accepting school within the neighbourhood. This then creates its own tensions in the league tables. Two schools serving the same area may have pupils gaining greatly different results in SATs. This is apparent across phases, but is more so at primary level as pupils attend schools within their neighbourhood. It skews the tables in favour of the academic achievements at one school over another. Without looking more closely at the ethos of, and possibly more holistic approach to, the education of children of the more inclusive school, it appears in an unfavourable light against its close neighbour. These tensions are not yet resolved and the goodwill and level of professional relationships are unquantifiable factors that support the inclusive process with pupils with special needs.

> There has been much confusion over what is meant by disabled children being truly included in an ordinary school. This is not just related to the physical environment where disabled children are expected to be as mobile as possible without the school buildings being changed or the lack of provision of personal assistants, communication aids, Braille and computer equipment. It is also how disabled children are valued as learners by non-disabled people. Inclusive education should create opportunities for all learners to work together. This requires a recognition that learning is enhanced when individuals of different abilities, skills and aspirations can work together in a joint enterprise. (Barton 2001:129)

Supporting pupils with complex needs in inclusive environments

In November 2001 the DfES published *Inclusive Schooling: Children with Special Educational Needs*, which provides guidance on the practical operation of the new statutory framework for inclusion. By referring to inclusive environments, it is implied within the semantics that community facilities are built in order to be accessible and welcoming to all members of that community. The use of a facility by pupils who have very complex learning difficulties should have the necessary access facilities for this section of the community among its resources. Those resources should be in place to make development of a learning programme a task that is within the scope of a group of creative and flexible educationalists.

Within the same process of access should be recognition that the needs of these pupils are so complex that a necessarily high ratio of adults to pupils is necessary for success; also that these pupils come as smaller groups is an important factor to recognise when looking at criteria for the success of a facility. Numbers are not as important as fulfilling a range of needs that are presented by each pupil. This needs to be pointed out to the strategic managers who fund the use of such places. Changes in the criteria for successful use is necessary for pupils with complex needs.

> Consider pupils with learning difficulties, disabilities or disadvantaged in any way as first and foremost learners and work to create the most appropriate educational environment for each individual. (DfES 2003: 102)

By devising a way in which pupils can access a mainstream facility, in terms of learning opportunities, not just physical or curriculum access, they become fully included in the thinking and planning of the future role of the centre. It is a two-way process of exploiting the potential of pupils and staff of both school and centre as well as the centre itself.

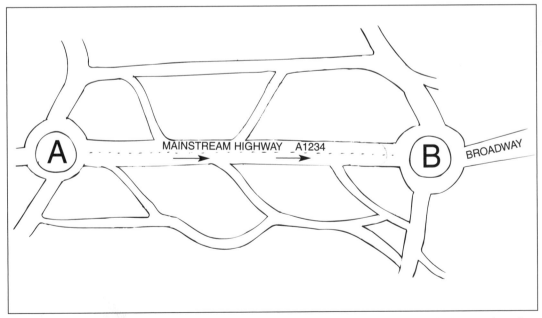

Figure 1.1 There's more than one way to get from A to B...it's all about planning ahead.

Inclusive education should create opportunities for all learners to work together. This requires a recognition that learning is enhanced when individuals of different abilities, skills and aspirations can work together in a joint enterprise. The education system has a responsibility to create learning environments and provide teachers who are skilled in creating ways in which all contributions are recognised as being of value. (Barton 2001: 129)

I suggest that, alongside this, there is the belief that learning environments can be developed to enable access to all as long as the personnel are accommodating and well-supported with funding to produce and promote a fully inclusive centre.

CHAPTER TWO

Excellence in Cities: an opportunity to do something new

The development of CLCs and their role in increasing opportunities for pupils to access the curriculum via the use of technology

Excellence in Cities (EIC) established City Learning Centres (CLCs) as a key instrument to deliver on four core values: setting high expectations of every individual pupil and all young people; developing diversity of provision; establishing and supporting networks of schools; and providing more opportunities to bring success to every school. As one of the local education authorities (LEAs) involved in the first phase of EIC, our challenge was to bring together the collective promise of learning mentors, learning support units, CLCs, more Beacon and Specialist schools, EIC Action Zones and extended opportunities for gifted and talented pupils as a powerful force for creating new and innovative learning opportunities for all youngsters.

Our CLC had a mission statement of 'learning at the heart of our community'. Our aim was to use ICT to remove barriers to learning. We valued each centre user as a learner – enabling them to access knowledge and skills at their own level. All our staff were considered as learners too – and although we helped, encouraged and supported, we did our best to remove the 'teacher' and the 'school' label that many pupils and older learners found off-putting. We were very much aware that many adults (some parents of our visiting youngsters) had negative memories of school days, and the last thing they were likely to do was to return to develop their ICT skills in a school environment. We worked closely with local companies, charitable organisations and voluntary groups to provide facilities for ICT training. Again, there was a need to develop a 'feel-good' factor about coming into the CLC to learn. The environment, atmosphere and ethos had to be right for learners of all ages, all subjects and all starting points.

The CLC learning environment oozed innovation, high-tech ICT and freedom to learn. The cyber café provided a much-valued area for sharing ideas, chatting, surfing and dining. We held a lot of our planning meetings in there – quite deliberately – because we wanted our visiting pupils and adults to know that we too had to plan what we did and to discuss and share ideas to do so effectively. All our visitors came into the cyber café for breaks. Pupils, community users, teachers and business users mixed together, passed each other when moving to their learning zone, and saw evidence of each other's work in the photographs used to document achievement. We celebrated the learning of everyone who came into the centre: those studying about bikes had their 'biking mad' photographs on the wall; we recorded still and digital images of students involved in F1 challenge when they raced the cars they had designed using the CAD/CAM facilities down our 80-foot track; visitors to the centre walked past an electronic welcome board indicating who the daily centre users were. Time and time again we exemplified 'learning at the heart of our community' in the way we welcomed all our learners, encouraged them to learn together and celebrated their achievements.

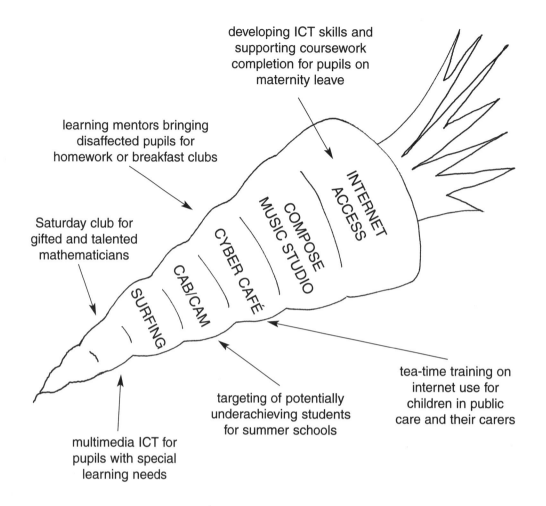

developing ICT skills and supporting coursework completion for pupils on maternity leave

learning mentors bringing disaffected pupils for homework or breakfast clubs

Saturday club for gifted and talented mathematicians

INTERNET ACCESS

COMPOSE MUSIC STUDIO

CYBER CAFÉ

CAB/CAM

SURFING

multimedia ICT for pupils with special learning needs

targeting of potentially underachieving students for summer schools

tea-time training on internet use for children in public care and their carers

Figure 2.1 The carrot? A quality learning environment!

In the early days of CLC development, when we first opened our doors, we spent a good deal of time inviting schools, community groups and LEA colleagues to experience the value of the facilities. We consulted with our local groups to establish courses and workshops that they felt were needed and would be likely to attend. The local primary school subject co-ordinators were invited to talk to us about areas of the curriculum they would like support to deliver. For example, Information and Communications Technology Co-ordinators struggled most when teaching multimedia and robotics to their older pupils (age 10 or 11). So we developed two programmes – one for multimedia, the other for robotics – during which pupils came to us for a series of workshops, taught by a member of staff. Our aim was to provide exemplars of teaching for the staff in school so that they could go back into their own school to teach the unit of work more effectively next time. We were not about developing a dependency culture – we did not want to teach either unit to all pupils in the area – and we did not want schools coming back year after year to cover the same work. Schools were encouraged to meet with the CLC staff beforehand to plan a multimedia or robotics programme that fitted in with their own curriculum, resources and network capacity.

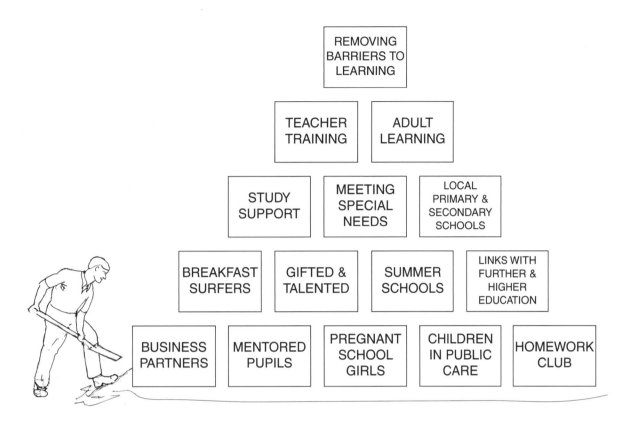

Figure 2.2 Building an inclusive environment

For several schools, our staff actually went to meet co-ordinators in their own schools to offer more individual support and advice. Schools were encouraged to send a range of staff to the workshops, along with the pupils, so that they could learn alongside the youngsters. When the unit of work came up again for them, we hoped that they would be able to teach it independently. We intended to move on – fully expecting to be providing something completely different and even more innovative in a couple of years' time. Our major focus was staff development.

When teachers and trainers came to the CLC, they came with differing degrees of experience and confidence. Some positively salivated as they entered and could immediately see the potential of our kit for their own teaching and learning. Others wanted to use the equipment with their youngsters but lacked the skills or confidence to do so. We developed a system of support for centre users, providing assistance at three different levels. Level 1 users came to the CLC requiring most support. In other words, they needed to be allocated a members of our team for the duration of their visit. Such users might be a teacher bringing a class for a demonstration lesson, a trainer from a voluntary group requiring network adminstration support and help to use the interactive whiteboards or an individual user coming along for a personal introduction to using the internet. Level 1 user time had to be allocated carefully because of the obvious high level of staff support time required. We always aimed to move our Level 1 users to Level 2 as their skills developed. Such users would be allocated someone to 'pop in' or be on hand to provide support when required, but would be expected to lead their own session or work independently. Level 3 users operated independently, knew our system and were confident to train, work with groups or operate independently. We could just hand over the swipe card to the room knowing that they were able to use and respect the kit within. We could accommodate many more Level 2 and 3 users in the CLC. Therefore it was in everyone's interest to have a simple and efficient network system and a programme of skill development. There was nothing more rewarding than one of our regular users declaring that they were 'OK on Level 3 now!'

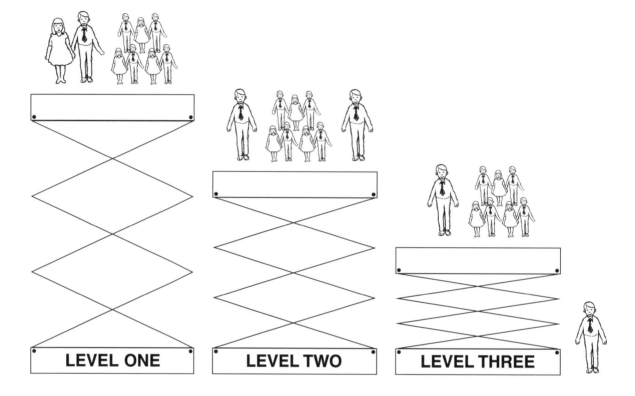

Figure 2.3 Levels of support offered to users in the City Learning Centre

At the time of carrying out the pilot inclusion project, the CLCs were new and, initially at least, we could easily find the time to discuss and develop the curriculum. In the early days we spent a good deal of time talking to groups supporting a wide range of youngsters who were becoming disengaged from the education system and were in danger of becoming lost to learning. Therefore we focused on providing opportunities for underachieving and vulnerable groups. For example, we prioritised room bookings and CLC staff support time for pupils from across the LEA who were on maternity leave via one day each week focused on developing ICT skills; we developed the ICT skills of 'looked-after children' and their carers who attended early evening sessions on using the internet and incorporating cartoons and clipart into birthday cards for each other; and we ran summer schools targeted at pupils with talent for music technology and design, introducing them to powerful software able to make the most of their talents, with teaching activities presented by strong and positive role models in the form of students from local colleges. We worked closely with Learning Mentors from a range of schools who brought their youngsters into the centre to motivate them, keep them focused on producing coursework assignments or to reward them for reaching their targets for achievement, attendance or behaviour. We provided that 'bit extra', and the buzz of learning was tangible.

We also worked closely with groups of gifted and talented youngsters who came along with their teachers during the day, after school and at weekends for extra workshops to stimulate their minds and take them beyond the learning possible within a full, mixed-ability classroom. Although not usually disaffected, such groups contained some pupils just eager to learn more and others frustrated that their hunger was never satisfied in school. A regular Saturday morning group of primary mathematicians thrived on the extra attention to their needs, both emotional and academic. A rather nice spin-off from this was that parents and siblings often came along to the cyber café and 'surfed' while the class was on. This gave the centre's staff the opportunity to chat with them, help them to get used to using computers, learn about the safe use of the internet at home, and how to access any further training if they wanted. Some sessions were run entirely by the CLC and offered to all local schools; some workshops were planned by schools and we supported them by providing some training and teaching; and for others, we merely provided the facilities and equipment. The centre worked with talented designers, musicians and artists. Pupils were identified as gifted and talented within primary schools, and secondary schools taking such youngsters on in year 7 were eager to keep up the momentum for learning, making it fun and 'cool'.

It was in this spirit of inclusion of all learners that we forged links with our partner's special school for the Interactive Multimedia ICT pilot. Our inclusive culture was developing, and a natural extension of this was to consider how we could improve our provision for pupils with special educational needs. We decided to start with a group of youngsters with the most profound and multiple needs – but who seemed to respond very positively to learning through ICT. We were developing a good relationship with staff from the school, so the time was ripe to consider how we could work with a partner special school to develop our curriculum and resources to meet their learning needs.

City Learning Centres: the technology available

Technical overview

The City Learning Centre's vision revolved around the use of state-of-the-art ICT to achieve the objectives described previously. The term ICT encompassed not only the use of computers and networks, but also a whole host of technological devices and apparatus, most of which were either unavailable or in limited supply in schools. The remit was not to provide equipment and resources to support curriculum provision – other initiatives were to take care of that aspect – but to facilitate out-of-the-ordinary learning experiences and those which extended above and beyond the 'normal' curriculum scope to which children were regularly exposed.

Equipment, such as high-quality digital still and film cameras, was available to support innovative projects across all key stages of the curriculum. The availability of this equipment allowed the team to think creatively about the application of these technologies in the education of pupils involved in the Interactive Multimedia project. The combination of capture devices such as these and interactive whiteboard technologies and data projection (available as standard throughout the Centre) opened up new horizons for the facilitation of learning for our pilot group. Pupils could be filmed and, concurrently, could watch the footage live on a large screen. This enabled children with poor fine and gross motor skills to participate in the activities, without having to try to see into a small viewfinder. Similarly, linking the output of a still digital camera, which was operated by a switch, to a data projector allowed the pupils to line up, judge and execute their own photography with little or no intervention from the adults involved.

The use of professional audio post-production equipment, such as the Air FX sound-making unit, a recording studio complete with digital mixing desk and state-of-the-art software allowed pupils to record their own sounds, create new ones, store them digitally, and then alter them using software synthesisers. Again, the fact that the equipment was digitally based allowed many of these operations to occur via the use of large switches, and in other ways to increase their accessibility, and to break down the inherent barriers to learning which would have been ever-present without creative use of the equipment available.

Large numbers of computers and high-quality output and printing equipment meant that there was always the facility to individualise the experiences according to the particular child's needs; using data projection for some, switch access for others, or touch-screen technologies for those whom it benefited. The large conference room had excellent rear projection presentation facilities which allowed the finale of Unit 3: 'Communication' to be carried out with real panache. The pupils each presented the outputs of their experiences to an audience of fifty or so invitees, and there was a palpable sense of excitement and achievement as each pupil went through, mostly unaided, their favourite film clips, sounds and photographs.

The availability of high-specification video and sound-editing facilities, along with professional quality multimedia authoring software allowed the creation of the final CD-ROM record of the pupils' experiences, which were used as both a record of their achievement and as source material for further reflective experiences back at school.

However, as well as being excited at being able to offer this level of technology to a wide range of users, we were aware that this may also appear intimidating to the user with less-well-developed skills. We made every effort to make people feel comfortable in the Centre, through layout, decor, and person-to-person, but we felt that it was also necessary that users felt that they were stakeholders in the CLC and not just users. Therefore, all new users were registered at the start and given a unique user name and password. This gave them access to the network resources available at the Centre as well as their own reserved space to save work and use it for their own personal files. There were no generic or guest user names at the CLC: everyone knew that they were valued individually, not just as a usage statistic. They were also given passes to operate the electronic security doors which protected the expensive equipment against intrusion. This way, they felt welcomed and trusted. All of these operation strategies were designed to make users feel as much a part of the CLC as possible, which, in turn, boosted confidence in their own abilities to succeed.

The technology available allowed free thinking in terms of the possibilities for enhancing the experiences of the children, and allowed them to take ownership of their actions in ways which would have been difficult or impossible without them. However, that is not to say that it would not have been possible to provide these experiences with less-advanced equipment; more that the design and implementation of the pilot was greatly expedited by it. Most, if not all, of the learning opportunities can be reproduced using equipment available in most special schools, and, indeed, this was a consideration through the design of all the activities.

The City Learning Centre technologies provided a platform not only for the inception of the project but also for the training of other teachers, and a mechanism for the dissemination of the good practice. The involvement of the City Learning Centre was crucial to all these facets of the project.

CHAPTER THREE

Team building and collaborative working

In the early days of opening the City Learning Centre, we invited a range of school staff, local businesses and community members to visit to share the vision we had for providing alternative and innovative opportunities for learning. This was our mechanism for getting to know our local learning community. We formed a good relationship with staff from local schools who began to use our facilities for staff training, exemplar teaching workshops and after-school and holiday activities for pupils. Many groups quickly saw the potential of the City Learning Centre and we were approached to provide the venue and training for a wide range of innovative, more bespoke learning opportunities for staff and pupils. The cyber café became an informal meeting place as relationships developed, and it was here that the seeds for many of our projects were sown.

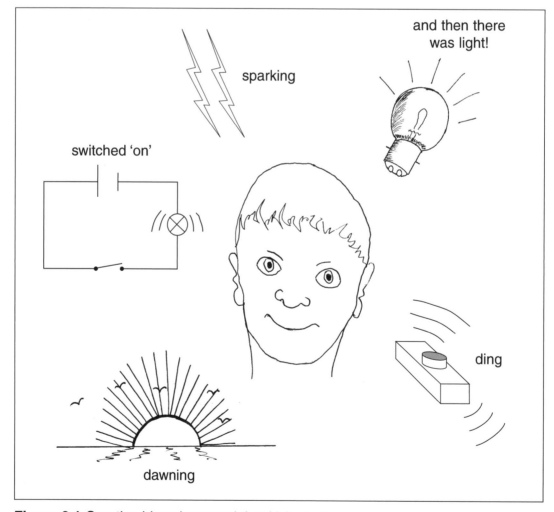

Figure 3.1 Creative ideas just need that kick start

The early discussions about an ICT inclusion project were held between City Learning Centre staff and an advanced skills teacher from a special school about five miles away. Although some of the team members knew each other and our work, we had never actually worked together before. Having said that, knowing each other's views on inclusion and having formed a positive relationship before we started the project gave us the confidence to be sure we would work well together in future.

The City Learning Centre had nine different learning zones (as described in Chapter 2). We talked about the potential of each zone and how appropriate it would be for an inclusion project. It was clear, early on, that in order to have a meaningful discussion, we had to have an actual group of youngsters in mind because the needs of each class within the special school varied so much. We chose a group of five Key Stage 4 students with profound and multiple learning difficulties, some of whom had already shown a positive response to learning through information technology. We wanted them to go into the cyber café for their breaks and lunch and to be able to mix with other learners, both adults and pupils. We recognised the importance of the sensory aspect of their curriculum and the potential resource provided by the computers, digital cameras, music studio and conference suite. The City Learning Centre was equipped with state-of-the-art specialist kit, and the sheer range and number of resources was well beyond the budget of any typical mainstream school. This kit was being used by a wide range of mainstream youngsters and training adults. We wanted to extend its use to make it available to students with the most severe learning needs. It did not take too long for us to realise that if we could combine our kit with the special school staff and pupils we had a potentially strong partnership and a unique opportunity to put together a Key Stage 4, age-appropriate ICT curriculum experience as an inclusion project.

Project management

There were three stages to our project. The first stage was the scoping exercise, part of which we have already described to you. We identified the project, those to be involved and the level of commitment required in terms of time and resources. We also put the stages of project development on a timeline and calculated the resources demand. By the end of the scoping exercise we had a draft project plan which we could share with our 'stakeholders'. In other words, we had worked our ideas into something concrete that we could present to those we wanted to work with. This included staff, pupils, parents and LEA officers. The plan was particularly important from the point of view of the Centre and the school. Both the manager and the head teacher needed to be able to timetable pupils, allocate teaching and support staff, and fund or acquire the right resources. We needed to know the scope and limitations of what we were getting into.

The second stage of the project was to implement the plan. The plan involved:

- identifying an appropriate group of pupils;
- determining how long the project should last;
- planning the curriculum units of work;
- identifying the resources required including time demand and funding;
- identifying funding sources;
- identifying success indicators, mainly quantitative and related to pupil progress, but also relating to the transferable nature of the project;
- planning for evaluation of the impact of the project, against the success indicators; and
- dissemination of good practice.

The third stage of the project was to use the evidence gathered from the evaluation of the project to decide whether to work with a further group of stakeholders to extend the learning opportunities to other pupils and other schools. Time was needed to reflect on what went well, and what didn't; what we would do differently and the ideas we would use again in the same way.

The role of project management was taken, in the main, by the City Learning Centre manager. A close working relationship with the advanced skills teacher from the special school provided a very effective communication route between the Centre and the head teacher in the school. The head teacher and advanced skills teacher ensured that the project was implemented at the school end.

The project team

It was important for us to pull together a project team with the right combination of knowledge, understanding and skills. Equally important was the need to have team members capable of working together collaboratively. Let's take a moment to reflect on what that meant to our project.

We started as a group of three individuals with an interest in inclusion and a good idea for a project. The project team had a core of three individuals, namely the CLC manager, an advanced skills teacher for inclusion who worked at Penny Field Special School, and a teacher adviser from the CLC. We each had strengths to contribute to the project, and, most important, we were all committed to sharing what we knew with each other and learning from each other. When it came to considering how the team would operate, it was quite productive to clarify what we did not want to do, rather than being sure about what we did. We did not want 'experts' to swoop in, carry out specific tasks for us and then leave our team without passing on their expertise. By the end of the project we each fully intended to be more aware of the full spectrum of inclusion issues and be able to take our new knowledge, understanding and skills to other groups of pupils and school staff. Figure 3.2 illustrates the range of areas of knowledge and expertise to be covered during the project.

Figure 3.2 Project requirements in terms of knowledge, understanding and skills

We needed to know what we could bring to the project ourselves, and in order to add further value to the potential learning of our trial group, how to include others who would augment our contribution. We took time to identify the 'knowledge, understanding and skills' required for the inclusion project and we identified four areas of expertise. These were:

- inclusive education;
- ICT curriculum;
- human resources management (including buildings); and
- ICT resources and management.

We established a planning team of three, and involved others with specific skills to support us. The project planning team consisted of the Centre manager, an advanced skills teacher from a local special school and an ICT advisory teacher who also worked at the City Learning Centre. The following sections explore the knowledge, understanding and skills within the team and how we put them to use during the project. We also discuss the other staff who became involved in the project, the knowledge, understanding and skills they brought to the project, and the role they played in ensuring its success. It is worth saying at this point that whatever we came to the project with, by the time it was finished we were all far richer for the experience. The City Learning Centre had 'learning at the heart of the community' as its motto – and we all considered ourselves to be a learners as well as project deliverers.

We identified the need for team members to have a thorough, practically based understanding of the inclusion of pupils with profound and multiple learning needs within a specialist centre. The advanced skills teacher with responsibility for inclusion brought a deeply held belief in the value of inclusion, a thorough understanding of the principles of inclusion and experience of adapting the curriculum for pupils with special educational needs. She provided a strong link with the special school, communicating effectively with the head teacher and ensuring that efficient arrangements were made for pupil transport, medical needs, meals etc.

It was natural that the advanced skills teacher led on this area, supported by the CLC manager. Both understood the national agenda (DfES 2000) and signed up to the increased inclusion of youngsters. The advanced skills teacher for inclusion worked in a school with a strong inclusive culture. In her school, the curriculum was already enhanced by a range of opportunities to work in mainstream primary and secondary settings. She was experienced in planning, teaching and supporting such sessions. She also worked closely with LEA inclusion staff to keep them briefed on the work of the school and to advise on projects in other schools.

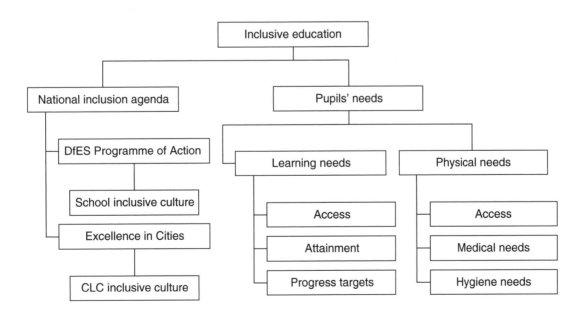

Figure 3.3 Knowledge, understanding and skills relating to inclusive education

The advanced skills teacher knew the children in her school well, and thoroughly understood their learning and physical needs. She knew immediately which class would benefit most from being the trial group for the project. She was able to clarify their previous learning experiences and present levels of achievement using 'performance descriptors'. From this we could discuss the level at which the learning objectives within the planned unit of work should be pitched. This helped enormously in planning for appropriate resources, levels of staffing and the focus of staff activity in the classroom. When the project was running, she worked collaboratively with the advisory teacher on short-term planning and team-taught each lesson, sensitively guiding the match of activity to pupils' learning needs.

The advice and guidance provided by the advanced skills teacher extended to the pupils' access needs including moving around the building to get to different learning zones, such as COMMUNICATE for video editing (which was on the first floor) and COMPOSE for music recording and editing (where the editing suite was smaller than the live room, and we had to move equipment around and place it wisely in order to ensure the whole group could access it). We also responded to the need for hygiene facilities, utilising disabled facilities within the Centre and also the hygiene suite within an adjacent school building.

The CLC manager had set up a centre in which inclusion was valued and was becoming embedded within its culture. Excellence in Cities focused on bringing about a step change in standards in an inner-city area. The CLC embraced that principle on behalf of all learners, including those with the most severe learning needs. The CLC also focused learning opportunities on pupils who faced a wide range of social or learning disadvantage as well as the gifted and talented as described in Chapter 2. A natural extension of our work was to provide a learning experience for pupils from the special school.

When youngsters visited the CLC for a learning activity, particularly one that involved a series of sessions, their learning culminated in a celebration event. This was always held in the CONFERENCE suite. A large screen, able to display presentations, TV, video and video conferencing, was available, and operable by the simplest switch mechanisms. This principle was applied to the youngsters from the special school who delighted parents and carers, other pupils, governors, staff and LEA representatives as they confidently took the audience through a presentation of their achievements.

The CLC mission statement related to 'learning at the heart of the community'. The Centre welcomed learners of all ages and abilities throughout the day, into the evening and during weekends and school holidays. It was intended that learners mixed during their time at the Centre, so youngsters and adults could expect to pass each other on their way to the training session, drink hot or cold beverages together during morning or afternoon breaks and eat together at lunchtime. The CLC staff were encouraged to consider themselves as learners, attend training sessions and work collaboratively to share skills and expertise. All visitors to the Centre benefited from learning together. The students from the special school were encouraged to get to know the Centre and to use all the social and learning facilities alongside other visitors. The students were to meet and be greeted by all the staff, and they thoroughly enjoyed getting to know them. We made as many of the learning zones and equipment as we could available for use.

Table 3.1 The match of knowledge, understanding and skills with the core project team staff in terms of inclusive education

INCLUSIVE EDUCATION Project knowledge, understanding and skills	Team members		
	Advanced Skills Teacher	CLC Teacher Adviser	CLC Manager
Project management	✓		✓
Pupils' learning needs	✓		✓
Pupils' physical and medical needs	✓		
CLC vision and ethos		✓	✓
Special school vision and ethos	✓		

The project team understood inclusive practice and how to interpret the principles appropriately within our partnership. Our project focused on providing youngsters with an inclusive environment within which to learn about ICT.

As far as this inclusion project was concerned, the project team members could offer the knowledge, understanding and skills relating to inclusive education. However, it is good practice to disseminate to others, particularly in a newly developing area of education. Therefore we involved a wide range of Centre, school and LEA staff, discussing what specialist provision we would make available to the students during the project, and the resulting progress in learning we anticipated.

The celebration event at the end of the project provided a valuable opportunity to show learning in action, and a wide range of stakeholders were invited. Parents and carers saw at first hand the facilities their children had used and the strides in learning they had made. Other staff, children and governors also acknowledged the students' work as they watched, laughed and clapped during the performance. LEA staff present provided a vital link between this project as a one-off event and the development of a longer-term strategy for the inclusion of pupils with a wider range of special educational needs in this and other City Learning Centres.

Since the project was to be based within a City Learning Centre, it was natural that we should focus on a Key Stage 4 unit to deliver an appropriate section of the ICT National Curriculum. As for all curriculum areas, the team needed to thoroughly understand the relationship between the National Curriculum and differentiated forms of this to provide an appropriate curriculum for pupils with profound and multiple learning needs.

The team needed to take on board all the best practice associated with planning learning objectives pitched at an appropriate level of challenge for each student in the group. We needed to understand 'performance descriptors' and the progression inherent within them. We also needed to understand when and how to assess pupils with the most severe learning needs. Evidence of learning outcomes manifests itself in a range of ways, and not only did our team need to be aware of these, but we also needed to train CLC staff and school staff to spot pupils making progress, particularly in the ICT skills they were developing.

The keystone of effective differentiation is the cyclical relationship between curriculum planning and assessment. Understanding progression in learning is central to being able to plan effectively. In ensuring that knowledge of the youngsters' prior learning and level of attainment determines the pitch of the learning objectives for each lesson, we are inevitably assessing based on prior attainment. Quite simply, we cannot plan without having first made an assessment, and in order to assess, we must understand the progressive steps that represent learning.

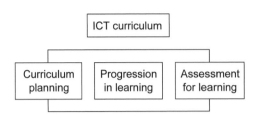

Figure 3.4 Knowledge, understanding and skills relating to ICT curriculum

The CLC manager had extensive experience in curriculum planning for primary, secondary and special school pupils. Both the CLC manager and the teacher adviser had a thorough knowledge of the ICT curriculum. Together they utilised this knowledge to creatively interpret guidance (QCA 2001) on Key Stage 4 ICT for pupils with learning difficulties. They were responsible for identifying digital imagery, digital sound and digital communication as a medium for teaching about 'controlling devices'. All pupils were to be given the opportunity to explore different sources of stimuli and information; for example, videos of themselves and sounds generated from musical instruments and electronic 'noise makers'. A series of short, focused tasks was planned within each unit – for example, taking photos of people and ICT equipment. A longer integrated task was required, and the perfect opportunity for this was incorporating a host of photos, videos, sounds and linking symbols within the individual celebration presentations. This partnership was vital in determining the curriculum focus of the inclusion project.

The CLC manager had worked with special schools in the past and had led the production of 'TRREACLE', a practical model for planning for and assessing the learning of pupils with special learning needs (Singleton 2002). This model provides a user-friendly approach to determining the progress of pupils working towards National Curriculum level 1 by identifying steps of progress. The advanced skills teacher was experienced in planning for and assessing pupils with the full range of special educational needs. Once we had identified which elements of the ICT curriculum we should focus on, the CLC manager and the advanced skills teacher worked together to produce an initial scheme of work for digital sound. The template found within QCA schemes of work for Key Stage 3 (QCA 2000) was used as a writing frame. Each scheme was to include exemplification of standards, links with basic skills, learning objectives, activities and learning outcomes. The model scheme of work for digital sound was then used by all three members of the project team to write future units on digital imagery and communication. These schemes of work can be found within Chapter 4.

Planning the curriculum for the project illustrates the importance of team working. All three members of the project team were involved in developing the curriculum. The team developed the curriculum in three stages. First, the CLC manager worked with the teacher adviser to focus the units of work on specialist areas within the City Learning Centre. Then the manager worked with the advanced skills teacher to write an exemplar

Table 3.2 The match of knowledge, understanding and skills with the core project team staff working on the ICT curriculum

ICT CURRICULUM Project knowledge, understanding and skills	Team members		
	Advanced Skills Teacher	CLC Teacher Adviser	CLC Manager
Project management	✓		✓
ICT curriculum planning		✓	✓
Progression in ICT learning	✓		✓
ICT curriculum planning for pupils with PMLD	✓		✓
ICT curriculum assessment for pupils with PMLD	✓		✓

unit. Finally, the CLC manager worked with the teacher adviser to write the remaining two units, guided by the advanced skills teacher who advised on the needs of the pupils with severe learning needs. We worked collaboratively, sharing our expertise, and in doing so we learnt a great deal from each other.

The team contained members with the right expertise to be able to plan the project curriculum, but we were not always going to be present during the sessions, and we intended that some activities would be carried out in school. Therefore, we planned to ensure all staff involved in the project knew the purpose of the lesson, their role in carrying out the activity and the anticipated learning outcomes. Sometimes staff were expected to encourage a pupil to anticipate an event, such as a particular sound, or to make a choice, for example, between taking a digital photo of a computer or a printer. It was important that staff knew which questions to ask, when to stand back and wait for the pupil to respond and when to take the lead. Prior to, and during, each lesson, the advanced skills teacher supported staff from her school by explaining the rationale behind the planned activities.

The CLC housed tremendous ICT resources for learning. The Centre welcomed several community groups, some of which supported learners with moderate learning difficulties. However, given the fact that the Centre had only just opened and was focused on introducing itself to the local learning community, until we started discussing the inclusion project less thought had been given to its use by students with profound, multiple and severe learning needs. Figure 3.5 shows a summary of the knowledge, understanding and skills relating to ICT resources and their management that we considered the project team would need.

The advisory teacher was a source of inspiration when it came to the creative use of ICT for learning. His personal knowledge of the workings of ICT was well balanced by his commitment to teaching others how to be confident users of ICT. He ensured staff could use basic ICT equipment such as digital cameras and video. He became proficient quickly in using video-editing software and using the network within the Centre to display images on whiteboards and within the CONFERENCE suite. He chose appropriate software for pupils to use when generating and manipulating sounds. He was creative in his choice of interactive presentation software for the presentation to parents. Chapter 5 focuses on which ICT resources were used and how they contributed to the project curriculum.

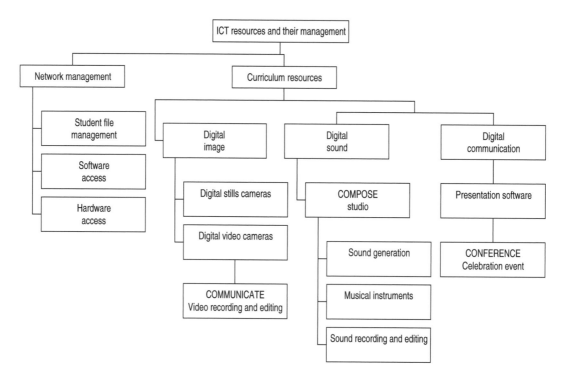

Figure 3.5 Knowledge, understanding and skills relating to ICT resources and their management

The CLC teacher adviser had already delivered some ICT training to the school staff prior to starting the inclusion project, and had developed a good relationship with the school. He went on to provide further training specific to the project focal areas of digital imagery, digital sound and digital communication. Staff were given training to develop their own skills and to enable them to repeat or practise activities back at school. He showed the teaching staff how to use ICT hardware, such as digital stills and video cameras, so that they could use the equipment with students in the CLC and reinforce developing skills back at school. The Centre was able to loan some kit to the school to support this. He trained staff on the use of sound generation devices within the CLC's COMPOSE studio and showed them how to capture and manipulate the sounds with pupils. Staff were also trained in using the presentation software and hardware for our grand finale – the celebration event – as the culmination both of the unit on digital communication and the pilot project itself. A good relationship had developed based on the first round of school-based INSET. The staff valued the training given and thus had faith in our capacity to prepare them for the project when we suggested it.

The teacher adviser was involved in delivering the school's New Opportunities Fund funded ICT training, ensuring that all staff were able to update and develop their own ICT skills and capabilities. He worked with the advanced skills teacher to practise the skills required to operate digital cameras and sound equipment prior to each lesson. He also provided additional on-the-job training for additional teaching and support staff who attended lessons with the pupils. He worked collaboratively with the school staff to teach all three units to pupils when they attended the Centre.

The City Learning Centre benefited from the ICT wisdom and inspiration of several colleagues working in schools and for the local education authority. The original design rubric enabled the development of superb learning zones providing the potential for learning in different ways, such as through the CYBER or COMPOSE studios. We were able to discuss specific access hardware for our group with profound, multiple and severe learning needs with the special school staff and other special school senior managers in the city; and to secure funding through Excellence in Cities to purchase touch screens, big switches and flexible ICT trolleys.

Table 3.3 The match of knowledge, understanding and skills with the core project team staff working on ICT resources and their management

ICT CURRICULUM AND THEIR MANAGEMENT Project knowledge, understanding and skills	Team members		
	Advanced Skills Teacher	CLC Teacher Adviser	CLC Manager
Project management		✓	✓
Resource identification and acquisition or prioritised booking		✓	✓
Access hardware and software	✓	✓	
Visual image hardware and software, e.g. digital stills and video cameras		✓	
Video recording and editing (Communicate)		✓	
Sound generation, recording and editing (Compose)		✓	
Interactive whiteboard technology		✓	✓
Presentation software		✓	✓
Presentation Event (Conference)	✓	✓	✓

Within the CLC we had staff who, although not involved with the project on a day-to-day basis, made their own contribution. The network needed to be utilised effectively to set up accounts, passwords, secure personal folders and to transfer new files containing images or sound files ready for the next session. Staff within the Centre always had their finger on the pulse when it came to new and innovative software packages, and we opted to use a particularly simple but effective version for our celebration presentation.

By working closely with a wide range of stakeholders, we made the project better. We consulted, listened, learnt and implemented using the views and ideas of a range of 'experts' (none of whom would probably have ever claimed to be such) to make use of existing equipment to its full potential, make wise resource purchases and to be brave enough to do things differently.

A strength of our project team was that it was made up of CLC staff and a member of staff from the partnership school working in close collaboration. The smooth running of the project depended on our team's effective communication with other staff from the special school and within the Centre itself. From the CLC perspective this was quite simple – the manager was a member of this team and was therefore able to make plans to manage the deployment of staff and other resources. Liaison with the school was potentially more complex. The first hurdle was to convince the head teacher of the value of the project and the role the City Learning Centre would play in improving the learning opportunities for her students. We were fortunate in that the head teacher was proactive in seeking inclusion opportunities and valued the work of both the CLC and the advanced skills teacher from her own school. In many ways, we were pushing against an open door and the project team benefited enormously from the support and encouragement provided by the school management and staff.

We established a strong communication link with the school in the most natural way – via the advanced skills teacher who worked closely with the senior managers to keep them informed of both the project demands and progress. This link was equally effective in ensuring we engendered the support of the governing body; gained permission from parents and carers; and thus, most significantly, secured prioritised timetabled time for staff from the school to join us for curriculum planning, teaching sessions and project evaluation. We identified suitable individuals or groups and began the process of describing our project to them and explaining the areas we would appreciate support in. It was important to come to a common understanding about the degree of commitment, in terms of the time, and number of meetings and deadlines. In order to convince them that the project was worthwhile we had to be very clear about the learning gains we expected from pupils and the professional development we would provide for staff.

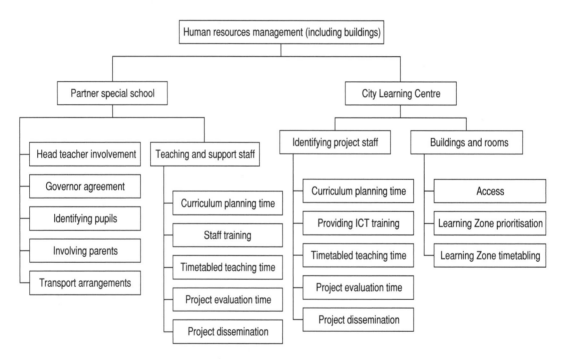

Figure 3.6 Knowledge, understanding and skills relating to human resources (including buildings)

Figure 3.6 shows the breadth of human resource management undertaken during our inclusion project. To be honest, the full extent of this element of our work was only truly appreciated when we reflected on everything we had to ensure was organised in order to run the first series of workshops.

In order to start to explain what we did it is useful to consider the role of the partner special school and the City Learning Centre separately.

The advanced skills teacher from the special school played a crucial role in the project team by providing that vital link between the Centre and the school. She worked closely with the head teacher to gain the commitment of the whole school, including governors, to taking part in the project. She worked with her teaching colleagues, explaining the focus and aims of the project, and how the school had identified the group of youngsters most likely to benefit. With the support of the school she went on to obtain parental/carer permission for their involvement. In requesting permission, we had to be clear about the purpose of the project and the nature of the activities to be undertaken. Because of the nature of the planned units of work, we also had to ask permission for photographs and video images to be captured, stored on the network and embedded within presentations. We intended each student to leave the project with a CD for later use at school or home. Within this could be photographs of other students in their group. All parents/carers agreed to their children taking part in the project, and the vast majority agreed to photographs of their children being taken. It was important that we ensured the wishes of all parents/carers were respected. Therefore, care was taken to provide a range of opportunities for students to take permissible photographs of different objects and individuals. Practically, we ensured that some of the class were photographers rather than subjects; and photographs of some youngsters were used in the short term, not stored on the network and not reproduced or embedded within the files of others.[1]

The project required regular, sustained commitment from the school. This commitment was in terms of arranging for minibuses and drivers, and timetabling students, teaching staff and teaching assistants. Parents/carers had to agree to their children attending the Centre for a half-day visit each week for two terms. The project was valued as an inclusion pilot by the local education authority and the school secured funding for supply staff to cover classes, enabling others to be involved as part of their continuing professional development.

School staff were involved in the project in a range of ways. The project team produced draft schemes of work and shared these with the class teacher to fine-tune learning objectives and plan how activities would be delivered. Curriculum planning sessions were held at both the school site and the City Learning Centre, some during the school day, others at the end of the day or in lunchtimes and non-contact periods.

The CLC also had a human resources management role in supporting the project. Having the CLC manager as a project team member was a major advantage. Being completely sold on the combined potential of ICT and an inclusive setting for learning, there was an immediate commitment to prioritised time for curriculum planning, timetabled sessions and project evaluation. However, this did impact on the overall work of the Centre and had to be timed appropriately. The Centre opened in autumn term 2000. The purpose and management arrangements of the Centre are described in Chapter 2, but briefly, the CLC had to work with 60 schools, plus community members and businesses, in an identified geographical 'wedge' of the city to provide new and innovative learning opportunities, removing barriers to learning. The initial priorities within the CLC development plan revolved around engaging wedge stakeholders (one of which was the future partner special school). The inclusion project was therefore incorporated into the development plan for implementation during the following spring and summer terms.

The CLC manager worked as a project team member and also co-ordinated the staffing, and the room and resource bookings within the Centre. The CLC ran a flexible booking system that enabled Centre users to access resources with one of three levels of support, varying from Centre staff running exemplar lessons for teachers with their pupils (Level 1), through to groups coming along with their own teacher and using spaces and resources independently (Level 3). The philosophy behind encouraging users to move from the intensive support offered (at Level 1) to independent working (or Level 3) is described in Chapter 2. Co-ordinating the booking system with staff timetabling was crucial in order to ensure teaching and technical staff were available when required. It was useful to identify and prioritise a specific session for our inclusion work. Tuesday morning became inclusion project time. For a couple of weeks at the start of the term this time was used for curriculum planning and training before becoming the reserved time for youngsters visiting the Centre as a class. The CLC teacher adviser was booked to teach and support the class throughout the project. Any time beyond this had to be found once school users had left or when independent groups were in the Centre.

At the same time as prioritising staff to support the project, the CLC manager ensured that appropriate learning zones were made available. This included prioritising access to some specific zones, such as COMPOSE for digital sound activities; CONFERENCE for observing video and digital images on a huge screen; and CYBER for free-surfing, dining and between-lesson 'chilling' sessions. This was more complex than just booking a room for each lesson. One of our inclusive principles was for our students to mix with other Centre users, have time to experience the Centre's hustle and bustle, use open and quiet areas for learning, and use ICT for specific learning activities and for recreation. Some rooms were on the first floor, requiring youngsters to use connecting corridors via the lift in the adjacent school building. Practically, staff had to be trained on managing access, such as emergency evacuation procedures and appropriate access routes for wheelchair learners and those with limited mobility.

The final, and most crucial, involvement of staff from the school was in evaluating the impact of the project. We had taken a half-day per week for two terms from the school and we were duty bound to show what we had achieved with it. Project evaluation was carried out either during the teaching sessions, by grabbing time with visiting staff, or by the advanced skills teacher for inclusion who spoke with her colleagues back at school. This was yet another advantage of having a project team member based at the partner school. We also met together as a project team to identify what went well, what didn't, and how we would do things better next time. The evidence we gathered was used to evaluate the project to advise the local education authority on its potential for dissemination.

In evaluating our work, we had to be clear about our success criteria and how well we had met them. We decided that impact was measurable in two ways: first via pupil achievement; and second, the transferability of our work to other school and specialist settings. Impact was most easily, and immediately, determined by the value added to the learning of pupils. To determine this we used school teacher assessments against national performance descriptors as our baseline, considered the targets for achievement set by the school and measured the progress individuals made. Chapter 4 details the teacher assessment outcomes and provides anecdotal evidence of progress evident in the responses pupils made to the activities. We could clearly show the extent to which students' learning had been enhanced by ICT and an inclusive environment.

Potential impact in terms of transferability to new settings was harder to measure, and indeed would only be evident in the longer term. We had a duty to ensure similar opportunities were made available to other youngsters and staff. We were mindful of the project principle of not involving 'experts who would swoop in and leave'. The last thing we wanted to do was to carry out a great project, with evidence of substantial impact on pupils' learning, and then not enable others to replicate it. The next stage for us was to take all the feedback from the school and Centre staff, pull out the effective aspects of our work, learn from our mistakes and draw up a development plan to disseminate our work around the local education authority. This plan was to involve a wider range of special schools, a couple of mainstream schools designated as specialist provision and other City Learning Centres. Chapter 7 focuses on the dissemination of good practice and will guide you through the production and initiation of a three-year project plan to be implemented within the local education authority.

Table 3.4 The match of knowledge, understanding and skills with the core project team staff working on human resources

HUMAN RESOURCES (including buildings) Project knowledge, understanding and skills	Team members		
	Advanced Skills Teacher	CLC Teacher Adviser	CLC Manager
Project management	✓		✓
Pupil selection and parental involvement	✓		
School teaching and support staff deployment	✓		
CLC staff deployment			✓
CLC learning zone timetabling and access		✓	✓
Securing time for curriculum planning, assessment and evaluation	✓		✓
School to CLC transport arrangements	✓		

The project team members had to have, between them, a wide range of knowledge, skills and understanding. This expertise was always enhanced by the involvement of other individuals or groups in some way, never more so than when it came to managing how and when to involve staff, parents and governors. In a way, we could have omitted this paragraph, because involving others is implicit within a section on managing human resources. We didn't though, because it is an opportunity we would like to take to say 'thank you' to everyone who gave of their faith, time and intellect to making this project the success it was. Quite simply, we couldn't have done it without the full commitment of staff from the partner school and CLC, parents, governors and the local education authority.

Note

1. It is also worth noting at this point that all photographs taken complied with general guidance and good practice in terms of how subjects were framed within images, guidance on working with looked-after children and the publication of images in promotional material etc. Further guidance on can be found within Chapter 5.

CHAPTER FOUR

Writing schemes of work

This chapter focuses on how the inclusion project team developed schemes of work suitable for pupils with severe, profound and multiple learning needs. The writing of schemes of work can be an emotive subject. Teachers are all too aware of the hours devoted to planning schemes of work – some of which have operated for one school year only – the only blessing being that if you write the scheme yourself you really understand it. Experience of working on curriculum planning in a wide range of schools tells us that, no matter how original, unique or locality-focused the activities in our medium-term plans are, the bulk of ideas will be very similar to those planned by our colleagues in previous years, in a school down the road or in another part of the country. So there has to be a happy medium to be found between writing schemes every year so that we understand them and the merits of an accepted set of medium-term plans upon which colleagues in a school can base their short-term plans for their specific class, knowing that units of work build on previous experiences taught by colleagues in preceding years. The national schemes of work produced by QCA (1998, 2000a, 2000b) reinforce the principle that long-term plans show how units of work may be distributed throughout a key stage to provide continuity of experience and progression in learning. Medium-term plans exist for the medium term; they are there as a framework to be modified, developed and personalised to a school's needs – a continuous process of refining until major National Curriculum changes shift the goal posts. Short-term planning is exactly that – for the short term. Teachers adapt medium-term plans to suit an individual, group or class for one lesson or a series of lessons within a unit of work. Short-term planning formats and processes are co-ordinated at an individual school level.

The principles of long-, medium- and short-term planning are becoming embedded in school planning. The long-term plan plots the curriculum journey pupils will take by plotting units of work, linked to the National Curriculum programmes of study, to be taught over their time in a key stage or across the whole school. Medium-term plans detail the appropriate learning objectives for each year group, the range of activities resourced by the school and the learning outcomes. We are not short of materials to look at when it comes to writing school schemes of work – quite the opposite. Schools now all have access to nationally produced schemes of work; websites providing curriculum planning guidance and examples, published schemes of work and, most probably, a host of resources generated over the years by colleagues and now stored in filing cabinets. Sometimes the most difficult task curriculum planners face is sifting through the vast range of materials to decide which ones suit our pupils best, and which ones do not.

Curriculum co-ordination in schools operates in a range of ways, and the differences are not just related to phase. Some co-ordinators in primary schools write schemes of work for the subject(s) they are responsible for, to be used by staff from Foundation Stage through to year 6. In other schools, individual teachers produce their own schemes of work for all curriculum areas for their year group. And there are a host of systems with elements of both these, such as individual key stage co-ordinators producing Foundation Stage, Key Stage 1 or Key Stage 2 schemes for all curriculum areas; co-ordinators for literacy, numeracy and ICT producing whole-school schemes; and individual teachers producing class-specific schemes for other areas such as history and art. Secondary schools operate a similarly vast range of systems for curriculum planning. Department or faculty structures may include key stage co-ordinators who produce schemes of work for year groups within Key Stage 3 or 4. Some operate a system where teacher specialisms are deployed enabling individuals to lead on the production of schemes for particular aspects of the curriculum. In some departments, groups work collaboratively, commonly utilising the expertise of both newly trained and longer-standing, experienced colleagues as sounding-boards. As I write this, I know that some of you will be thinking that the way you manage the production of schemes of work in your school is different from all models mentioned. Worry not! There is no single 'best' way to manage curriculum planning – but two important principles should be borne in mind. The first is that all schools, whatever the phase and whether specialist or mainstream provision, can be expected to share a common notion of curriculum planning structures. Secondly, however your school manages the planning process, its effectiveness will be determined by how well the curriculum is monitored for delivery by teachers, evaluated for impact on the learning of pupils and modified for improvement by subject co-ordinators and school senior managers.

Curriculum planning has moved a long way, particularly since 1998, when national schemes of work were produced. Not that these schemes solved all our problems – I am not suggesting that. What I am suggesting is that there is now a model format, providing a very clear message about expected levels of details within, and longevity of, long-, medium- and short-term planning. This chapter will not detail the principles of good-quality school curriculum planning – there is enough guidance on that in documentation from QCA (1998, 2000a, 2000b) and primary or secondary national strategies. I will focus on how we used existing models of quality planning to produce schemes of work for use with pupils with a wide range of learning needs within the City Learning Centre.

Translating planning guidance for mainstream schools into a special school situation (SCAA 1996) reinforced the principle of long-, medium- and short-term planning. However, it is vital to acknowledge that the curriculum for pupils with profound and multiple learning difficulties must be broader than the National Curriculum (and Religious Education). Schools are encouraged to consider priorities beyond such statutory curricular provision, including areas which require policies and therefore curriculum provision, e.g. careers education (DFE 1994); areas a special school has chosen to develop policies and curriculum provision for, e.g. health education, information technology, communication; and particular school priorities within the curriculum, e.g. physiotherapy.

The City Learning Centre manager identified the need to develop quality curriculum planning that exemplified national best practice and was instantly recognisable and understood by partner schools. We aimed to have City Learning Centre curriculum planning documentation that would be seen as good practice by visiting schools, local education authority advisers and Ofsted inspectors; and we adopted the principles of good planning from QCA (1998, 2000a, 2000b). As a result, schools recognised our workshops as useful because the titles and content matched their long-term planning for the delivery of units of work. Table 4.1 provides an overview of our long-term planning.

Table 4.1 Overview of long-term planning for Inclusive Multimedia ICT

School year	Curriculum Units	Staff involvement
AUTUMN 1	Curriculum Planning (2 weeks) Staff Training (2 weeks) Unit 1 Digital Sound	CLC staff/AST All School staff KS4 Support staff
AUTUMN 2	Unit 1 Digital Sound Unit Evaluation and planning for next unit (1 week)	CLC staff/AST KS4 Support staff
SPRING 1	Staff Training (2 weeks) Unit 2:Digital Imagery	CLC staff/AST KS4 Support staff
SPRING 2	Unit 2: Digital Imagery Unit evaluation and planning for next unit (1 week)	CLC staff/AST KS4 Support staff
SUMMER 1	Curriculum Planning and Staff Training (1 week) Unit 3 : Digital Communication	CLC staff/AST KS4 Support staff
SUMMER 2	Unit 3: Digital Communication (culminating in presentation) Unit evaluation Project evaluation Planning the roll-out programme	CLC staff/AST All School staff KS4 Support staff

The medium-term planning formats we used contained the same sections as those exemplified within national schemes of work. Although schools' planning formats differ, and some do not use the QCA format, most include the same section headings, such as learning objectives, activities and learning outcomes. Therefore, we had a shared understanding of what constituted quality curriculum planning and a common language to use with partner schools when discussing the fine detail of how sessions could be differentiated in the short term to suit the learning needs of specific groups of pupils during their visit.

The project team comprised staff with a good deal of expertise in curriculum planning. The CLC manager had been a school improvement adviser, primary and secondary school inspector and had supported curriculum development in numerous primary, secondary and special schools. The CLC teacher adviser was involved in delivering ICT curriculum training for primary and secondary school staff. In Chapter 2 we discussed how the City Learning Centre established a good relationship with local schools by inviting subject co-ordinators to local meetings to demonstrate the potential of the facilities and to invite a discussion about the role the Centre could play in supporting curriculum delivery. Prior to meeting any partner schools, the Centre staff had to be clued up on all curriculum areas and topics schools are expected to deliver within each key stage. In collaboration with our local schools we identified where the Centre's resources could contribute to each subject area and planned a CLC curriculum to match. The inclusion project was no different. One of our regular visitors was the advanced skills teacher for inclusion who was quick to spot the learning potential for her students. We began to look at how the Key Stage 4 programme of study (DfES/QCA 1999a) and national schemes of work for information and communication technology could be adapted for a group of 15-year-old (Key Stage 4) students, using the City Learning Centre's resources. The advanced skills teacher was experienced in all aspects of special school curriculum planning, and thus became the third member of our curriculum planning team.

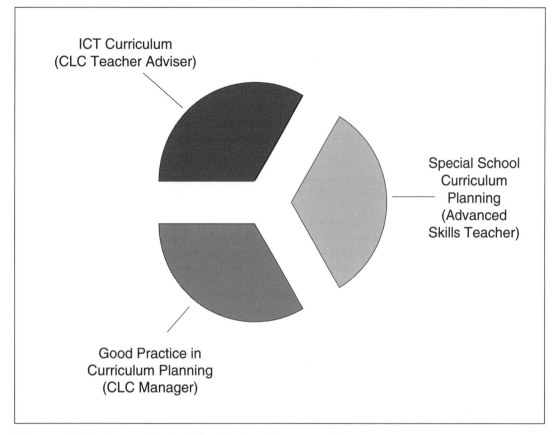

Figure 4.1 Inclusion Project Curriculum Planning Team

We started with the National Curriculum for Information and Communication Technology. In line with the common requirements in the National Curriculum Orders, we selected material from an appropriate key stage programme of study and planned to teach it in an age-appropriate way. Working closely as a team, we brought together appropriate elements of the National Curriculum for ICT; the school's policy on curriculum provision, communication and access; and the City Learning Centre's potential to provide different learning opportunities via state-of-the-art ICT equipment. Guidance on planning for pupils with learning difficulties (QCA 2001) identifies opportunities and activities for pupils in Key Stage 4, with a focus on using ICT tools with increased independence to produce and present work; using ICT in the wider world to control devices; and reviewing and evaluating their work and that of others.

We also looked at the guidance for pupils with learning difficulties in Key Stages 2 and 3, which provided a wider range of ICT-based learning opportunities and a clearer indication of how to pitch our teaching appropriately for each student in the group. Following the recommended model, we identified two levels of activity for pupils to engage in during each unit of work. These were: short, focused tasks; and integrated tasks. We then put this guidance alongside the digital imagery, digital sound and digital communications units we had in mind, and started the process of producing new, tailored medium-term plans.

Table 4.2 Opportunities, activities and approaches for pupils with profound and multiple learning needs, linked to the programmes of study for Key Stages 1 and 2

	QCA guidance for all pupils at Key Stage 4	Examples of short, focused tasks Pupils may:	Examples of integrated tasks Pupils may:
Digital Imagery	To experience and explore different sources of stimuli. They use the information to make simple decisions and choices and communicate them to others by appropriate means.	Observe digital and still and video images of themselves, other people and objects. Use ICT hardware to capture digital still and video images of themselves, other people and objects.	Produce a collection of digital images of selves, friends, staff and familiar objects from the ICT units. Select chosen images using icons and/or external switches.
Digital Sound		Explore sound-making instruments, e.g. drum kit, keyboards, digital sound-making devices. Choose preferred sound effects from vocal sounds produced by self or others in the group.	Choose sounds to be included in a compilation of sounds generated electronically or using a range of musical instruments. Select chosen images using icons and/or external switches.
Digital communication		Use printers to produce still images in colour and black/white for the A3 multimedia book. Use a range of external switches and icons to select print, save, menu etc. within a prepared presentation including familiar images of peers, parents, teachers and objects.	Select images and text from a range of work achieved to compile an A3 laminated book as a record of work done in the ICT units. Use a software presentation package to present work done to an audience of peers, parents and others.

This guidance is also helpful in identifying parts of the Key Stage 4 programme of study that are likely to be too challenging for our group of Year 11 pupils with profound and multiple learning difficulties. For Key Stage 4 pupils, such areas include:

- applying the concepts of ICT modelling;
- understanding the advantages and disadvantages of ICT;
- critically reflecting on the impact of ICT in their own lives; and
- using their initiative to exploit the potential of new ICT tools.

Looking at this list, it was quite obvious that our students with PMLD would not be able to access a curriculum demanding the application of concepts and critical reflection. As a curriculum planning team we needed to know both what to avoid and what to do to hit that button of 'appropriate pitch' when writing learning objectives and planning activities to deliver them. National guidance explicitly encourages us to cover only relevant aspects of the programmes of study. We were also clear that as long as the activities were age-appropriate, we could plan for learning experiences from within any key stage.

Our planning triad brought together three areas of expertise: general curriculum planning; an in-depth understanding of the curriculum for information and communication technology; and knowledge of the learning needs of pupils to undergo the programme. Most of the learning experiences we selected were derived from examples within units from the Key Stage 2 programme of study. Our next step was to ensure we differentiated appropriately. We did this by considering the range of learning objectives we needed to plan for. We started by looking at performance descriptors (QCA 2001) for information and communication technology. Some students were operating within P levels 1–3, where the steps of progress are generic and therefore applicable to any subject area. Other youngsters were operating at a higher level, and were capable of achieving from P level 8 up to levels 1 or 2 of the National Curriculum. In much the same way as schools are developing their curriculum plans over time, for the pilot project we developed medium-term plans to cater for the first group of students, with the intention of adding to them following an evaluation of the learning experiences we offered and the learning needs of individuals within classes who would follow a similar path in the future.

In line with QCA schemes of work (1998, 2000a, 2000b), each medium-term plan contains:

- an overview of the unit, indicating sub-units within the overall unit of work;
- where the unit fits in with previous experiences of both pupils and staff;
- technical vocabulary to develop with (staff initially, then) pupils;
- a list of recommended resources;
- expectations linked with performance descriptors; and
- sub-unit plans containing: learning objectives; teaching activities; learning experiences and outcomes; and points to note.

Learning objectives were pitched at an appropriate level either to encourage pupils to operate more securely at the level currently being achieved, or to move them on to the next level. Previous knowledge of the pupils cannot be stressed enough at this stage, not least because it takes a long time to get to know how much our pupils with such severe and profound learning needs are capable of.

A good deal of thought was given to how activities would be presented in order to present an appropriate amount of challenge. For example, during Digital Imagery, when pupils were asked to capture a still image using a digital camera, staff considered:

- whether students should capture an image using a large 'big' switch or the camera button;
- when to demonstrate camera operation – and when to describe it;
- when to provide a stimulus straight away and when to encourage anticipation and thereby recall of previous experiences;
- when to offer choices and encourage decision-making;
- when to provide instruction step-by-step and when to 'chunk' an action into a sequence consisting of several steps at once; and
- when to help the student use the switch, button, icon or movement sensor, and when to leave them to get on with it themselves.

The examples of different approaches within a single activity illustrate the importance of staff understanding the learning focus of the activity – that is, why the pupils are engaging in it – and what we really want them to get out of it. The temptation to help them to produce a visual image at the end, and the ease with which we could slip into 'doing it for them' needs to be discussed with both teachers and support staff. It is not the end-product that is important here; it is how the pupils were involved in getting there that counts.

The range of different approaches is also not merely a list of possible ways of carrying out an activity. As the list progresses, each approach represents a further step in learning. Each step provides an indicator of pupil achievement and thus progress. We linked our steps to performance descriptors. All staff were trained in planning for progression and in being aware of the challenge they presented to youngsters as they supported them through the activities.

We found it useful to exemplify how pupils may show the progress they are making during activities within the schemes of work. In order to make these memorable for staff, we used the TRREACLE (Singleton 2002) approach. To show how this would work, we can take the list of possible approaches above, and link it to performance descriptors. Table 4.3 provides examples of how staff could interact with pupils within the same class, using similar equipment, to enable learning from P1 (Tolerate) through to P4 (Link Experiences).

Table 4.3 Getting the 'pitch' right, in the way we present activities to pupils with profound and multiple learning needs (P1–P4)

Achievement level	Performance Descriptor	Presenting the activity with 'pitch' in mind
TOLERATE (P1.1)	Pupils encounter activities and experiences. They may be passive or resistant. Show simple reflex reactions. Participation is fully prompted.	Place students in contact with the activity. Lift a hand to trigger a movement sensor and thus produce a sound variation. Stroke the limb before movement. Talk about the limb being moved. Talk about the sound being generated.
REACT (P1.2)	Emerging awareness of activities and experiences. Periods of alertness and readiness to focus. Intermittent reactions.	As above, plus talk about the reaction made; praise the reaction; reinforce positive reactions; encourage a repeat reaction where appropriate.
RESPOND (P2.1)	Consistent responses to the familiar. Reactions to the unfamiliar. Begin to show interest.	As above. Encourage the same positive response to a stimulus. Introduce a modification of the stimulus with the same or different sounds being produced, e.g. moving the hand more slowly, or closer to the sound generator.
ENGAGE (P2.2)	Communicate consistent preferences and affective responses. Recognise the familiar, moving towards. Perform actions and learn responses over short periods of time.	Encourage pupils to move, or allow the movement of, limbs to generate similar or different sounds. Draw attention to other pupils moving hands over the sound generator. Ask pupils to repeat activities and reinforce progress, for example by commenting on sustained responses such as watching a hand moving or listening to a range of sounds.
ANTICIPATE (P3.1)	Remember learned responses over extended time period. Communicate intentionally, seeking attention through eye contact, gesture or action. Observe results of own actions with interest.	Ask pupils if they remember what they had to do to generate a sound. Give an opportunity for pupils to recall and communicate what the sound generator did. Comment positively on attempts to anticipate or eagerness to take a turn. Give lots of opportunities for pupils to observe previously experienced hardware and to recall what it did and how they had to interact with it to produce a response.

Achievement level	Performance Descriptor	Presenting the activity with 'pitch' in mind
CHOOSE (P3.2)	Emerging conventional communication. Greet and initiate interactions and activities.	Encourage pupils to choose between different sound generators, different musical instruments or order of turn-taking. Focus on making choices and creating opportunities for pupils to initiate interactions. Let pupils decide when to move to a new instrument, which equipment to photograph or which photograph of music hardware or instruments to place within their file.
LINK EXPERIENCES (P4)	Know certain actions produce results. Intentionally make selections to communicate meanings or outcomes.	Ask pupils to follow instructions, gradually moving them from step-by-step copying to several steps and towards learning a technique – such as making a range of sounds with a sound generator. Encourage recall over longer periods of time and increasing independence in choosing techniques to make sounds, e.g. via instruments or computer-generated sound and preferred sounds in terms of pitch, volume and mix.

The schemes of work in Chapter 6 further illustrate how the performance descriptors were used to plan for progress from P1 through P8 and on to levels 1 and 2 of the National Curriculum by clarifying our expectations of pupils making progress towards each stage.

Learning objectives were linked with learning outcomes as an indication to staff of how achievement and progress may be manifested during interactions with students. As the project was to roll out to a much wider range of youngsters with the full range of learning needs, we would develop the plans later to produce 'red (P1–4), green (P4–8) and blue (P7 – NC level 1)' routes as outlined in the Introduction. Much of the differentiation relied upon teaching and support staff modifying the way in which an activity was presented to provide the right balance between support and challenge. In order to enable all staff to pitch their approach just right, it was essential to provide training, not only in the ICT equipment and curriculum coverage but also in their role in allowing learning to take place.

We engaged our students by treating them like typical teenagers. We planned appropriately challenging, stimulating activities, and we had them using high-tech kit. Enquiry, experimentation and trial and error ensured engagement (of the staff as well as students!). Pupils took activities where they wanted to – mostly around taking more and more pictures and creating louder and more unusual sounds. Our curriculum, and the way we presented it, made learning fun. Our teenagers were motivated and made extraordinary progress. We had developed a powerful learning combination.

The pilot progamme

The special school perspective

Although the implementation of this pilot programme preceded the findings of the Special School Working Party by over two years, the planning, gathering groups of staff together, delivery using mainstream facilities and working together carry the same essential message: let's open the special schools for the benefit of the pupils educated on the sites and to benefit all pupils within both special and mainstream education, whatever their needs. The following Key Principles, underpinning the vision of the Special School Working Party, fit the view necessary for the successful implementation of such a programme and of the way ahead for those who work with pupils with special needs in any educational setting:

- to provide high-quality education and care for pupils in maintained, non-maintained and independent schools and demonstrate expertise in working with pupils with complex learning difficulties, behavioural difficulties and with sensory or physical impairments;
- to ensure effective partnership working between special and mainstream schools, the wider community and health and social services to meet the needs of children and young people and their families in a holistic way;
- to innovate in curriculum development, and develop different ways of providing effectively for pupils with a range of SEN, and facilitating their inclusion into mainstream;
- to have high expectations of all pupils with SEN and to raise levels of attainment and achievement;
- to provide resource bases for teaching methods, resources and ideas, for both special and mainstream schools;
- to be outward looking, seamlessly integrating specialist staff and SEN pupils into the wider community of schools;
- to include special schools in the full range of new policy initiatives coming from the Department. Policy initiatives will be specifically tailored for special schools – they should not be add-ons.

(DfES 2003: 5)

These may be their vision, but the

'last messages coming from staff, parents and pupils who took part in the Report conclude with the need for:

- high expectations and equality of opportunity for all pupils, wherever they are educated;
- breaking down the barriers between schools;
- celebration! Pupils were keen to have their aspirations and progress recorded, recognised and celebrated.

(ibid: 170)

All these points are covered within the programme as it was devised, planned, delivered, shared, evaluated and celebrated.

The school eagerly grasped the opportunity for pupils to access the new resources available. Senior management made it possible to release the inclusion co-ordinator to be part of the team alongside the class teacher and support assistant. The programme was given a high profile within the school and was regarded as a good way for the pupils to gain from using the new technology, and it had an added benefit of making the school the first special school in the area to use a City Learning Centre. Thus the pilot programme was seen in a positive light as a good thing for the whole school, not just the small number of pupils involved. The local education authority was approached for funding for the programme and echoed the school's enthusiasm for developing a scheme of work for the pupils, little realising the knock-on benefits for other special schools working with mainstream cohorts or in small groups in the specialist facility. The funding for the high ratio of staffing came both from the education authority and from the budget of the City Learning Centre. As the group of staff began to work closely together, the excitement of trading ideas and of seeing creative thinking transformed into technological reality that was accessible for all the pupils affected all. The programme became part of the school's inclusion agenda and carried the spirit of this in the message that all pupils, regardless of learning difficulty or educational need, could access and learn from being included in the work of the City Learning Centre. By starting with a group of Key Stage 4 pupils, the ICT National Curriculum was available for us to use as a basis for our planning. This sent an important message to mainstream schools – all pupils could grasp the challenge of the changes in learning styles brought by technological advances. Although these resources were designed for the majority to use, they could be adapted to benefit pupils with the most complex needs as long as the funding and the staffing were in place. Both finance and staff needed to be flexible in approach, willing to accept each other's ideas and the ideas of those staff not directly involved. This, ironically, included the school ICT co-ordinator who was not involved in planning or delivery of the programme, but who discussed the programme with those involved away from the situation and welcomed the great opportunity for staff development. So the programme opened up the opportunity for non-specialists in ICT. Creativity, the ability to share skills with other professionals, excellent communication skills and team working were the main ingredients that made the programme work and be highly successful in terms of pupil and staff learning.

The programme does need to be seen as a whole-school issue, as the benefits to other pupils in the school following the pilot were immeasurable in terms of ways in which staff viewed a much broader approach to ICT and how planning and delivery changed for other pupils. Without the support of the head teacher or the education authority, it is doubtful whether the programme would have had the impact for the other pupils in the school, or indeed for spreading the programme to other special school pupils and staff (see Case Study – Fairview School programme, Chapter 6).

Selection process for the pilot group

The school involved in the programme from the initial planning stage is one for pupils with severe and profound and multiple learning difficulties. It was decided that the pupil group used would be in Key Stage 4, for purely practical reasons. The rest of that group were out accessing inclusion in a mainstream school; the small group left had their class teacher, who knew them well and had devised their Individual Education Plans, and the school assistant, who also worked as part of that class team. The lead teacher from the school ensured that the staffing was intensive for this group of five pupils. Added to this were the lead Information and Communication Technology teacher at the City Learning Centre and the manager, who contributed time to planning and researching the programme. In spite of this apparent ad hoc arrangement for choosing the pupil participants, the range of needs within it were broad and would provide us with a diversity and challenge to test our powers of creativity in the use of the technology available.

Where the programme fits with the Report of the Special School Working Group

In the pilot programme were five pupils with a wide range of needs. All pupils had severe or profound learning difficulties with additional complexities of mobility, fine motor skills and sensory losses. Each one provided a challenge for the expertise of the diverse group of educationalists grasping the opportunity of working together. One advantage was that all the pupils were familiar with each other and were all in the Key Stage 4 age range. The programme improved opportunities for access and potential. Digital imagery became large-screen photography, video recording, selection and editing. Digital sound took place in the music recording studio where synthesisers, drums and keyboards harmonised with the pupils' own voices to produce recordings for editing. By using musical software the pupils morphed sounds, chose their favourites (notably the drums with this group) and helped to compile a CD-ROM and book of experiences and learning. The final CD-ROM included photographs, video, sounds and words that celebrated their achievements. The final presentation for the parents, friends, press, councillors and officers of the local authority was the highlight for the pupils and for the staff. We had done it as a team; the pupils had achieved highly, and they knew it, as did the audience invited to the celebration. The pride the parents had in their children, who each presented their own work, was palpable; the atmosphere in the room was one of quiet pride and joy. To be able to share in the success of their children as they celebrated in front of such an auspicious crowd compounded the pleasure.

Accreditation was an aim of the team for the pupils who completed the programme, but the national schemes did not fit with our aims for the pupils. We wanted the programme accepted as a nationally validated scheme of work for pupils presently educated in special schools or resourced in a mainstream school. We explored many different accreditation schemes, but none seemed to fit the aspirations of the staff for the pupils or for the programme. A nationally recognised certification would have been a bonus to the pilot group, but as the programme is used more widely, different establishments may want to register it with ASDAN or Open College.

Pupil achievement

The danger of writing about the achievements of individual pupils is in the possible attitudes of those critically evaluating it after the programme has proved to be a success. However, all the pupils surpassed our expectations in all sorts of ways. These are detailed below, to be read in the spirit in which they are written. We all celebrate the success of our pupils, and try to describe them without patronising their efforts or the understanding of the professionals who will read this book. The success of the learning opportunities harnessed by our group of willing volunteers were validated by school staff who had known the pupils in an educational setting for a number of years, and by parents or carers who are the acknowledged experts in evaluating their own children and their responses to different stimuli.

David

David has cerebral palsy. He uses a power chair and has limited use of his upper limbs, with limited fine motor control. He maintains his seated posture by propping on his elbows on a tray attached to his chair. He tires easily and finds social situations more difficult as he hits his mid-teens. He has verbal skills, but his speech is slow with impaired articulation that makes him reluctant to speak to adults new to him.

He was very curious about the environment and accepted the new surroundings quickly. His confidence was assisted by the presence of staff from the school who were familiar to him.

David took part in every area of the programme, as described elsewhere in this book. He astonished all of us including those who knew him well with his adaptability within the programme.

We assumed specialist large single press switches would be necessary for David to take photographs. We were wrong, David turned down the proffered switch and asked to have a go with the ordinary button on the camera. By setting the camera on a tripod at an accessible height and with adult verbal support, David pressed the button using his forefinger. He took photographs of all the pupils and the staff as well as the equipment he used. The adult worked under his direction to set up the camera in the position David wanted it and moved it as he asked until he was satisfied with where it was placed. For a pupil as diffident as David within social situations, he gained enormously from this level of autonomy within a mainstream facility and away from the small community of the special school.

Another success that was not considered when planning the programme was the effect on his posture of seeing himself on a large screen 'live'. Due to his major physical difficulties, David had spent years being directed to 'hold your head up', without fully appreciating what this phrase really meant. He had worked with video and mirror numerous times before, but suddenly, looking at himself on the big screen, David raised his head to midline, readjusted his whole body posture in his chair and beamed at the camera. This has created a permanent change in his seating and his view of himself. This unforeseen benefit for David's physical programme was celebrated by the health professionals concerned with his wellbeing and particularly by his parents. His independent eating skills gained a level of skill previously unattainable and his view of the world changed – as he could maintain his head midline his attention to visual stimuli improved.

Figure 4.2 . . . if you had shown me what you meant by 'hold your head up straight' I might have done it before . . .

Annabel

Annabel has severe learning difficulties. She has limited verbal skills supported by key-word signing. Her walking gait is jerky with frequent tripping and almost falling to the ground. She needs constant monitoring when moving from place to place. She is very excitable which can interfere with her attention to task, already limited by her learning difficulties. She is a very engaging personality and was quickly adopted as a challenge by the advisory teacher for ICT based at the Centre. Although the teacher has had very limited contact with pupils with severe learning difficulties before, he recognised that Annabel's needs meant adaptations to mainstream equipment would enable her to access the programme alongside her classmates. Our initial problem was Annabel's ability to turn switches on and off quickly and suddenly to gain attention, thus causing problems when other pupils were receiving individual tuition. By appointing Annabel as his technical support worker, he managed to engage her with equipment that would not interfere with the learning opportunities of others. She was challenged by the tasks set, and would settle briefly to problem-solving without direct adult contact. By being part of the group without constant prompting, the staff noticed her attending to the work of other pupils. Her programme was set up so she could always follow another pupil. This would give her confidence and some control over her input into the programme by following the model provided by one of her classmates. She worked with the ICT teacher, the more familiar adults playing a supporting and observing role. She produced original work on both the imagery and sound components of the course. The celebration was the climax of the programme and Annabel coped with presenting her work to the audience including her parents. It was the first time they had been able to enjoy Annabel's success. She had previously refused to take part in school concerts or even use a broader environment than that provided by home and school and the close community.

Ria

Ria has profound learning difficulties. She needs support to walk, or uses a wheelchair, and is dual-sensory impaired. Her limited visual and auditory skills make the outside environment an extremely confusing and unlimited space. She also exhibits behaviour problems including attacking adults who attempt to engage her in activities when she has other ideas and refusing to access offered equipment or move towards objects or places of interest. It took time for Ria to enter the room where the digital imagery was presented. She did not access using a camera, as her complex needs made it an unrewarding task for her. However, when we set up the camera to transfer her image onto the Smartboard, Ria was transfixed. The adults all worked silently through the programme with her, almost not daring to breathe in case we broke her concentration. This pupil, with such complex needs including being registered blind, was fascinated by her own image. During the first two sessions she concentrated on moving her arms and watching as her image reflected what her body was doing. She invited a familiar adult to join her on screen by gesture, and the adult imitated Ria's own movements, much to her delight. The most memorable moment of the whole programme for many of us was when Ria directed the technician operating the camera to show her new trainers on the screen. He pointed the camera at them, she saw her image on the screen and moved her feet to admire the trainers. Her level of communication astonished us all, including those who knew Ria well. The motivation caused by this element of the programme for Ria was astounding to us all.

When choosing the video shots for inclusion in the celebration presentation, of course there was a lot of footage of Ria. As everyone was watching, Ria began to pre-empt the actions she did on the screen. The sequences of arm movements, the directing the camera to her trainers, she remembered them all. The effect on her parents was astounding as they watched their daughter use skills they were not fully aware she possessed.

Figure 4.3 'Point that camera down here, these new trainers are worth seeing!'

Charlie

Charlie has profound and multiple learning difficulties. He has severely limited vision and hearing loss. He is a wheelchair user. He has no verbal communication and is learning a very limited number of on-body signs within his school routine. He has frequent fits, which leave him tired and unable to engage in tasks. He needs verbal and physical support to access the activities on the programme. In some ways Charlie was the greatest challenge to our planning and delivery as he needed lots of specialist input to encourage him to interact with people or with equipment. Charlie's response to his image was holding his head up and communicating his pleasure by heavy nose-breathing and body-stiffening.

It was the effect of producing synthesised sounds that made Charlie's experiences very special. He used the AirFX machine by hand movements, changing the amazing sounds he generated. By exploring the sounds with help, Charlie could produce a range of different auditory stimuli to please and delight him and the rest of the group. Although he needed physical guidance to access the machine, the smaller movements that created changes in the sounds were Charlie's own.

George

George has severe learning difficulties, although he has none of the physical or sensory problems that affect the rest of the group. He did have severe confidence problems and it took a lot of working through his insecurity concerning accessing the City Learning Centre. By the time George actually appeared with the group he had seen photographs of the Centre and met the staff in the security of his familiar special school. The ICT teacher from the Centre negotiated with George to design his own programme within the remit of the digital imagery and digital sound components the other pupils used.

George has verbal reasoning skills and could be challenged to take and print his own photographs. He worked on his learning outcomes for all the areas of the programme until the celebration, and the members of staff were prepared for George not to take part. He refused to run through his work when we were trying to work out timing for the different elements of the presentation, although he did watch the ICT teacher working at the control desk with his classmates. He watched as special switch access was set up for other pupils to use so that they were directly responsible for their own presentation. George did not want to take part until within the situation. As the hall filled with familiar and unknown adults, George decided he wanted to go first. He gave a great presentation including talking through elements of his work and how he had taken the photographs and printed them. The sounds he produced spoke for themselves. To summon up the confidence to interact with an audience surpassed all expectations for George.

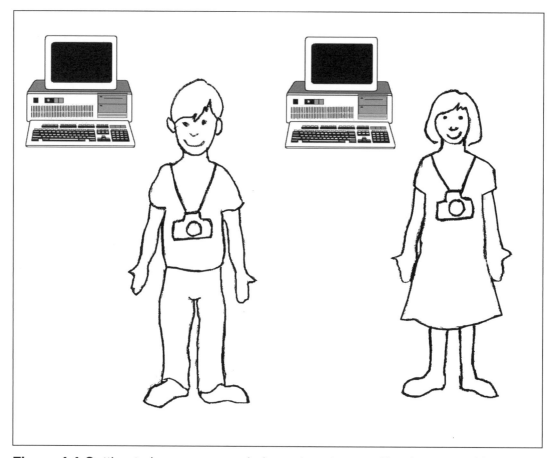

Figure 4.4 Getting to know new people is easier when we like the same things

Developments for other groups of pupils

Following the success of the project, it became apparent that more pupils could benefit from the experience of using the City Learning Centre using this programme. Other special schools have also accessed the programme in a similar way with groups of pupils with learning difficulties. The next challenge that presented itself was how to include the pupils with emotional and behavioural difficulties in a special school, who are excluded from mainstream school because of the disruption their presence causes to other pupils. The programme had already proved suitable for pupils with a wide range of abilities to access at their own level, with all suitably challenged by the work programmes. That the school for pupils with emotional and behavioural difficulties had no access to the expensive and latest in technology meant that accessing the resources the Centre had to offer was to become part of their educational entitlement and not an activity to be regarded as a privilege to be withdrawn if pupil behaviour warranted such sanctions. It was to be regarded as a right and not a privilege. Sadly, due to rapid staffing changes, this was frequently out of the control of the teaching staff directly involved in the programme.

We were extremely fortunate to attract a student working on a doctorate who wanted to record, over time, the changes in the interaction between the pupils with severe and complex learning difficulties and those who would facilitate their accessing of the programme, who themselves exhibited severe behaviour problems.

That pupils who are excluded from mainstream secondary school due to behaviour difficulties would be accessing the resources for the pupils with severe learning difficulties was not previously well-documented. Putting together two of the most excluded groups of pupils with the intention that one group should be responsible for the learning of the others appeared to be fairly innovatory.

In planning that the adults would be facilitators, by setting up the learning conditions for optimum interactions between the pupils, the parameters of the programme were set. This had built-in expectations of the pupils' social behaviour. By giving responsibility for the learning and experiences of one group of pupils to the other group, it was intended that the self-esteem and confidence of all the pupils would be boosted within their different roles.

This planning remained fluid, as the pupil input was important to its success. By teachers working on the pupil suggestions for adding parts to the programme or changing it, the pupils realised that their input was vital to the success of the programme. The group took some time to learn about each other, but the EBD pupils began to take control of the learning environment and of making decisions on behalf of the group.

Broadly, the planning of ICT activities is similar, but an important difference was in the staffing. Despite having staff at the City Learning Centre who were familiar with pupils with special needs, more experience for new staff was a development issue within the programme. The new technical support worker hit the ground running with this programme. He had to learn the needs of the pupils on the spot, with support from the visiting teachers. That he coped from the beginning, and was an important part of the team to both adults and pupils in the group, shows how much attitude sometimes counts over experience. That he felt real pleasure at achievements of the group, and of individuals in the group, showed that being part of the team had certainly helped his professional development as well as the pupils' learning.

All the pupils worked well together, apart from one pupil on the autistic spectrum and with severe learning difficulties. The pupils understood his need to be seated away from the group and to join in when he felt it was the right time. This could not be imposed on him. Andrew did set up his own conditions to make himself feel secure within this very different situation where the possible variables were considerable. The group looked to each other's achievements and experiences to share in their successes.

Standards of behaviour were enhanced by the imposition of positive behaviour management. Also, working with adults who were unknown to the EBD pupils helped to keep them focused, through modelling and guiding the pupils with severe learning difficulties. An atmosphere of calm and co-operative working prevailed throughout the programme. The EBD pupils did not have peer pressure to gain attention through inappropriate behaviour leading to poor role-modelling for the other pupils.

Other programmes using technology

This scheme of putting together groups of pupils with behaviour difficulties and severe and profound learning difficulties was not new to the teacher working alongside colleagues from the different schools.

Notably, a programme of work had already been planned, implemented and evaluated using the sensory room in a school for pupils with severe and profound learning difficulties with a group of Year 6 pupils from mainstream school who were in danger of rejecting education. At the age of 10, these pupils already had a history of missing school involving educational welfare officers.

The pupils were paired with a pupil with complex needs and the task was for them to set up a visual and auditory programme to benefit their partner. To devise a suitable learning environment for these pupils meant that they needed to learn how to interact with peers who had no verbal skills. They had to use observation and early communication skills to find out which stimulus was favoured by their partner. This programme took a year to plan, develop, deliver and evaluate. The supporting member of staff from mainstream school was the learning mentor – another Excellence in Cities funding initiative – and the teacher from the special school who devised the original programme set up conditions to allow the pupils to interact in as natural a way as possible without adults becoming a barrier to the communication between pupils. It is this direct contact that is a vital part of inclusion. The peer learning and experiences alongside similar-aged pupils are invaluable for pupils already segregated by being in a specialist setting for most of their education. They break down barriers with some of the most difficult-to-teach mainstream groups by raising awareness of the needs of others. Within this programme, the expectations included raising self-esteem, better self-management of behaviour and a sensitivity towards pupils who may not have the necessary skills to communicate or interact easily. This led to the guiding pupils developing a series of switches for each of the pupils, working together as a group, discussing and evaluating the needs of the individuals. They were shown a variety of access switches, joysticks, rods and rollerballs to set up for their partner. They were very concerned that their ideas would work for their partners, thus putting the needs of the other pupils first. The last session was filmed and the video viewed by all the pupils who agreed that it could be used as part of a training video for teachers, governors, parents and student teachers. This showed the extent to which the pupils had grown in confidence in their own skills and relationships and confidence that others would share their good practice.

Within their own mainstream school situation, the children who worked with the pupils with complex needs began to operate as a group within class, where they had not done before. It was noticed that they initiated discussions in lessons, looking to each other for assistance when working and building good working relationships where there had been none prior to the partnership work.

CHAPTER FIVE

Developing ICT skills

There can be little doubt that the advances in technologies over recent years have had a profound effect on the way that everyday life is led. Communications, entertainment, commerce and vast numbers of other industries have reaped real rewards from the increase in efficiency and the new ways of working that ICT has brought about.

Education of any learner can be similarly enhanced, as can the teaching of that learner. However, this has charged teachers and other educators with the not inconsiderable task of integrating these new possibilities into teaching, and harnessing the power of ICT to deliver more rewarding and exciting learning opportunities for their pupils.

Despite a whole series of initiatives, and funding, there still remains a skills gap in the teaching professions which can hinder the process of this change and incorporation.

In this chapter, some of the issues surrounding the encouragement of ICT use in education will be explored, and some strategies for countering reluctance will be discussed.

Reasons for the application of new technologies to education

There are a wide range of applications of technologies to the education context. These range from administration, assessment, target setting, communication and others, to the immediate impact that ICT can have on the learning experience of a pupil.

ICT can do several things to enhance this. These can be basic in their scope, such as using a word-processor to produce work which is easily read and well presented, or using a spreadsheet to tabulate data and present it in the form of computer-generated graphs. There may be time-saving applications in the classroom, such as using electronic monitoring equipment to collect data in a science lesson, freeing up pupil time for other, perhaps more productive, activities.

More exciting, however, are the new opportunities that ICT can offer, and experiences which would not be possible to offer children without the application of that technology. These can include the use of internet communications and electronic mail to allow pupils to exchange information with their peers in other geographical locations; allowing pupils to explore concepts and situations via the use of computer models; allowing reluctant writers the opportunity to express themselves and explore their ideas via a different media, such as digital video; or the ability to realise concepts with the help of computer-aided design and manufacturing equipment.

It is this second category of ICT use – allowing access to learning experiences not normally available to children with learning difficulties – which formed the basis of this project.

However, the purpose of the project was not only to provide these experiences for this single group of children, but also to allow the wider dissemination of this practice so that as many pupils as possible could benefit from it. This meant that more teachers and support staff had to become confident users of ICT in this context, and this can sometimes prove to be problematic.

Types of ICT user

For the purposes of this discussion, ICT users can be categorised into three broad groups: the reluctant user; the competent user; and the confident user.

The reluctant user

There are many teachers who find the idea of incorporating ICT use into teaching and learning somewhat terrifying. At first, this can appear to be for a variety of reasons: 'I can't use technology, it just goes wrong whenever I touch it'; 'What if it goes wrong when I'm trying to use it to teach?'; 'The kids know more about it than me'; 'What's wrong with what I've been doing for years?'; or 'I just don't see the point'. However, there are probably only two real root causes of this reluctance: the first, and possibly most powerful cause, is a lack of confidence in their own abilities. Even the most proficient and inspiring teacher can feel as if they are powerless when confronted with the possibility of integrating technologies into their teaching. The second – and one which is possibly the easier to solve – is the genuine conviction that ICT can offer nothing new to the experiences available to pupils. Both of these can seem difficult to address, but we will look at strategies to overcome both shortly.

The competent user

This user is one who understands that ICT can enhance the learning of pupils and their own teaching, and understands that technology has changed everyday life and is not going to go away. They see it as part of their job to use the possibilities of ICT to give pupils in their care the best experiences that they can, and are willing, with the right level of support, to begin to integrate technology into their working practice. They will tend to approach the issue by thinking 'What do I need to do?' and will receive training and support to allow them to achieve whatever it is that they need to do.

The confident user

The confident user is a discerning and enthusiastic user of ICT who has become almost autonomous in their own skill development. Rather than looking to see how technologies and applications can help them to deliver exciting experiences, they have gone a step further and now look at new technologies, and consider how these can be harnessed to provide those experiences. While this distinction may seem minor, it is, in fact, fundamental to the process of integrating new and emergent technologies into the education context, where appropriate. These users readily share knowledge and skills with their peers, and have the confidence to enthuse others about the experiences that ICT can offer.

Clearly these are very broad generalisations, but most teachers can be identified as roughly fitting one of these categories.

To run the multimedia ICT project effectively, all adults involved need to have an understanding that the ICT can indeed help to provide new and purposeful learning experiences for the pupils, and have the basic competencies to enable the project to run smoothly. Inevitably, it may be that in duplicating this project, there will need to be staff involved who are currently reluctant users. There is, therefore, a need for the project team to have some strategies to counter this, and encourage the upskilling of all of the team's members.

Starting off: encouraging the reluctant user

Considering again the two broad reasons why a user may be reluctant initially, we shall start with the one which is perhaps easiest to address: 'I don't see the point'. With the seemingly endless stream of new ICT initiatives that have buffeted teachers during recent years, there is also often a feeling that either *everything* is to be delivered via ICT, or that ICT is simply being used to satisfy some spurious statistic or criteria.

It is vital that this issue is addressed near the start of our process; even the most evangelical ICT advocate will admit that at times it is simply easier to use pen and paper, and that ICT is not a panacea which will end all the difficulties in the learning of our pupils. ICT is a valuable and powerful tool, but only when used intelligently and, above all, where it is appropriate. If there is a better way of giving a child a learning experience which does not involve ICT, it would be preposterous to suggest that this was no longer acceptable, because there was no technology involved. It is a far better thing to experience a Caribbean holiday in person than it is to view images of palm trees and sandy beaches on a computer screen!

There is never an expectation that ICT will be used in teaching and learning at all times, and rightly so; the teacher and the learner are still the central and most important parts of the process; ICT simply allows new ways of enhancing the interaction.

When faced with a colleague who is a reluctant user, it is important to be ready with a clear set of examples which demonstrate the additionality which the use of ICT can provide; in this case in the context of children with severe learning difficulties.

Instance 1: Digital photography

In the case where a child has poor fine and/or gross motor skills, the possibility of them being able to independently select, compose and shoot images which are relevant to them is remote. Difficulties in manipulating small buttons found on standard photographic equipment, difficulties in holding the camera still, and even difficulties in being able to see what is in the shot through traditionally small viewfinders, will all prove to be very real obstacles to a child accessing this experience.

However, if the output of the digital camera is linked to a data projector, the image in the viewfinder immediately becomes vastly magnified onto a wall or screen. The pupil now has a far better chance of being able to see what the camera is pointing at. Add to this a switch to trigger the camera shutter, and a stand clamped to the wheelchair, and that child can now fully engage in a rewarding learning activity which would otherwise have been completely closed to them. One of the children in the pilot project found themselves to have skills in this area that they would never have otherwise discovered, and this has opened up a whole new area of interest for them, and widened their world experiences.

Instance 2: musical entertainment

A child who has very poor gross motor skills, and very little vision, responds well to music, and can express a preference for different pieces. However, these pieces of music must always be offered to the child in a prescriptive way; all that the child has the capacity to do is to respond to what they are offered; not being able to physically change the CD or operate the controls on the stereo prevents the child from making independent choices.

If a large selection of music is digitised, however, and this accessed through a switch-operated software menu system, any available body movement (be it limbs, head or anything else which is voluntary) can be used to make a decision. As the menu system rotates through the available tracks, a 10-second excerpt of each track is played. If the switch is pressed during this time, the full track will play. In this case, the technology has provided the child with the mechanism to make independent decisions about their own environment, without the need for moderation by another person, which has the potential to be misinterpreted.

In both these cases, you can see that the outcomes were either impossible, or far more difficult to achieve without the use of ICT.

Now that our colleague has seen that ICT can have a genuine positive impact on learning, there is still the issue of a lack of confidence in his or her abilities to overcome. It is extremely unlikely that any professional teacher lacks the basic abilities to master a new skill, such as the operation of a computer. However, with the complexity and wide range of applications that are possible with modern equipment, it is easy to see why it may appear that one needs some sort of massive intellect to fathom the secrets of the computer world. In fact, quite the reverse is true; computers and their operating systems are designed to be as easy to use as possible; all that is really required is for one to acquire some very basic skills, and to break through some of the metaphor and jargon which is popularly used to describe computer operations. Allowing the user to gain some degree of competency in these basic skills is crucial if they are to adopt ICT as a tool. Some training is inevitably involved here, but this need not be as formal as it sounds. A friendly half-hour with a colleague after school once a week is often all that is required to give a teacher that initial 'leg up' towards an increased confidence. There are other ways of making this learning seem less intimidating too. Encouraging colleagues to work together is an excellent way of doing this. Some people would advocate pairing up with an experienced user, but often it can be even more effective to have a pair of beginners working together, with support available when needed. This will avoid any possibility of one teacher having any feelings of inferiority, and losing interest. The realisation that you are not alone in the fear that you are less than competent can bring real relief, and free you to pursue training without fear of ridicule. Encouraging some simple ways of using ICT to enhance the teacher's normal delivery can also be invaluable in nurturing progress. Try getting the teacher to produce a worksheet for a lesson using text and photographs in a word-processor; the pride and sense of achievement the first time that this is done can be quite astonishing.

While it is beyond the scope of this book to provide a comprehensive basic skills training guide, there are a few key ideas which should aid anyone in their move from a reluctant to competent user of ICT in teaching:

- It is extremely difficult to damage a computer by any other means than physical force. Pressing the wrong key at the wrong time will not cause the hard drive to disintegrate in a puff of smoke; and anyway, if this does happen, it would happen whoever was using the machine and it is the job of technical staff to sort that sort of problem out.
- The computer software commonly used by everyone worldwide is designed to be easy to use, and fool-proof.
- It is very easy to get lost in terminology when listening to the language used to describe simple computer operations. Try to use easily visualised metaphors when describing what is being done on the computer; for instance, when saving a file. A 'drive' can be described as a filing-cabinet which holds digital data, instead of paper

data. Therefore, a 'folder' is a way of dividing the filing cabinet (drive) up into more organised parts, containing files, be they digital or paper. Files go into folders, which, in turn, go into drives (filing cabinets). Using simple metaphors in this way, and linking to concrete, real-world situations, will make the user's understanding of what they are doing far easier to acquire.

- When stuck with little idea of what to do to finish a particular task, think of a sentence that describes exactly what you are trying to do; then look at menu options in the application that you are using and try to follow your sentence through. For example: 'I need to save this file to a floppy disk'. Looking along the available menus, 'Save' is not there, but 'File' is. Under the File menu, you can see the word 'Save'; following this through takes you to a screen where you can select the floppy disk drive. It is this sort of logic which, once it has been assimilated into the user's thinking, will allow them to interact more comfortably and intuitively with the computer environment.

- There will always be a way around a problem, even if it seems insurmountable. Usually, a simple question to a more ICT-literate colleague will yield a simple result (along the lines of 'You just need to click here . . .'). Although it can be extremely frustrating at the time, the likelihood is that the next time the situation occurs, it will be solvable without so much as a second thought.

Once a teacher starts to gain these basic skills, with a little help and encouragement from colleagues, they are well on the way to becoming one of those competent users. This means that, with the correct level of instruction, they will be able to go into a lesson and replicate what they have learned, without intervention or a high level of support from anyone else. They have gained the skills to become competent users of ICT in their teaching and are fully able to deliver the activities in this book on their own.

How far have we come?

It is an important part of the process of becoming a competent user to keep confidence high. If a fledgling ICT user feels that they are not making sufficient progress, they will lose confidence extremely quickly, and it may become far harder to re-engage them than it was initially. Of course, it is unlikely that in actuality they are not making progress; it may just feel like that to them. To prevent this sort of loss of confidence from happening, it is important to be constantly appraising exactly what their achievements to date have been. If a user was reluctant to even enter an ICT room, and a short time later they are producing word-processed documents, this is, in fact, an enormous achievement, and it is always worth reminding them of that.

Once a genuine belief in a teacher's own abilities to master ICT has been engendered, they will be willing to take more risks, try new approaches and some of their own ideas, and the process of becoming competent will accelerate.

What next?

While it is sufficient, and commendable, that all members of staff working on the project have become competent users of ICT in teaching, it would be ideal if they then all went on to become confident users. The change between these two types of user is subtle, yet profound. A competent user is able to carry out ICT-based learning activities with groups of children, given good instructions and training. However, in time, the regular use of these skills will become second nature, and users will then begin to think of new applications of what they already know. This is the start of a paradigm shift in that user's way of thinking. Instead of finding the right technology to help them to carry out a specific task, the confident user will see a new technology or software package and begin to think differently: 'How can I use that technology to good effect?'

Moving a competent user to becoming a confident user requires far less intervention than changing a reluctant user into a competent one. This change must come about from the person themselves, and it is more of a natural evolution of their skills which brings about this change than the provision of any training. Exposing them to a variety of technologies, such as those at a City Learning Centre, will do much to facilitate this process. This is the sort of user who will be able to take the ideas in the interactive multimedia project, and mould, extend and enhance them into further exciting learning experiences for their pupils.

How rewarding it is on the day when a member of staff who would not previously entertain the notion of using ICT produces a lesson plan for a new exciting ICT-based learning activity, and the pupils in our schools can only benefit from this increase in skill and enthusiasm of their teachers.

Practical Guides

How to set up the session for interacting with live video

This activity involves pupils interacting with a live video feed of themselves, projected onto a large screen. The purpose of this is twofold:

- firstly, to allow pupils to explore their own live, moving image, and demonstrate that the information captured by the camera can be displayed by another device; and
- secondly, to capture video footage of this interaction to provide a resource for the next activity, and for inclusion in the Multimedia CD-ROM. Captured footage of the interaction will also provide a record for the later assessment of pupil progress.

Considerations

The equipment used needs to be both carefully selected, and carefully set up. A good-quality video camera is essential, and this should ideally be a digital video (or DV) camera. This will allow easy processing of footage later. If no DV camera is available, then a standard video camera will suffice, although this will add an extra stage to the video processing later on.

The video camera needs to be capable of live image output; this facility is available on all DV cameras, as well as the majority of standard VHS cameras. The live feed from the camera then needs to be sent via a suitable cable to the video input of a digital projector.

Setting up the room

With the video camera connected directly to the digital projector, you have effectively set up the screen as a large viewfinder for the camera. This enables pupils who would not otherwise be able to access the small viewfinder on the video camera to do so, as well as allowing the rest of the group to view the video feed too.

It is important that the camera be set up on a stable tripod directly in front of the screen. In this way, a pupil sitting down will always be in shot, and be able to easily view the images on the screen.

Although this is essentially a group activity, it is important to allow each pupil in turn to view and interact with their own image, and theirs alone. To this end, ensure that the seating arrangements in the room allow the camera to be focused on one pupil at a time, without any of the rest of the group being in shot. This requires a little advanced planning, and a big enough space to work in.

Lighting is also very important when shooting any video. Try to set up a situation where there is good indirect illumination on the pupil (i.e. bright light, but not shining into the pupil's eyes), but where this does not distract attention away from the images on the screen. Sometimes a well-lit room is sufficient, but if lamps are needed, try to shine them at walls or the ceiling so that the reflected light illuminates the pupil. This will produce better quality footage with which to work later.

In this set-up, each pupil, in turn, can be put into the 'hot seat', or their wheelchair can be placed in the correct spot, while allowing the rest of the group to take part in the activity.

Hints and tips

- In order to demonstrate the concept that it is the camera which is capturing the image, and the projector which is displaying it, first sit in front of it yourself. Ask the pupils to observe what happens on the screen when you move towards or away from the camera, or behind it. Ask them to predict what will happen if you put the lens cap on the camera lens, or turn off the projector.
- Allow each pupil enough time to explore the activity fully; around ten minutes each should be sufficient.
- When caught up in the activity itself, it is easy to forget that one of the aims is to record some footage for later use. Don't forget to press the record button on the camera for each pupil. Stopping recording while changing between pupils will make the later editing and compiling of relevant footage more simple.
- Careful observation of the whole group's reactions to the images on the screen may also lead to some good insights as to their level of understanding of the process, when someone else is on the screen.

Some observed outcomes

The effect that this activity can have on pupils is often quite astounding. Pupils have been observed experimenting with gestures and facial expressions (more so than with a mirror, as the image is considerably magnified on the screen), putting their arms out to explore the limits of the camera's field of vision, and some pupils have significantly improved their posture after observing themselves on the screen.

How to set up a session for watching recorded video

This session involves pupils observing the video captured in the previous session. The purpose of the session is to allow pupils to gain the understanding that video footage can be recorded, and reviewed at a later date.

This activity is best done at a later date than the last one. This allows the footage to be reviewed and edited by the teacher, and if some time has elapsed between the capture of the footage and pupils reviewing it, they are more likely to grasp the concept that the images are recorded, and not live as they were in the last session. If both the pupils and their teachers are wearing different clothes than in the last session, this will also enhance the effect.

Editing the footage

The footage captured in the first session should be reviewed by the teachers before it is used in this one. What you will probably find is that much of the footage is not useful, and may consist of long periods of time with nothing happening. If it is used in this 'raw' state, much of the potential impact that this may have on pupils can be lost, as they will lose interest quickly if nothing relevant is happening. To address these issues, it is wise to crop the video down to the most interesting and relevant parts. These should be where each pupil is interacting with the images on screen, as well as some footage where each is not, if this was the case during filming. Try to cut out any areas of the footage that you may have recorded when pupils are changing over, or the camera is being set up.

The actual process of editing video can, at first glance, seem daunting, and a bit of a 'black art'. However, this need not be the case; the process is actually remarkably simple once a little time has been taken to investigate it. Modern computers, which are running up-to-date operating systems (e.g. Windows ME, XP or Mac OS X), have the in-built facility to carry out basic editing of this nature on captured video. Downloading the footage to a computer is easy if you have been using a DV camera: simply start the video editing application on the computer (Movie Maker for Windows, or iMovie for Mac), plug the camera into either a Firewire or USB port (see illustrations below) and follow the program's instructions. Both these programs have tutorials or help files which take you through the whole process. If you spend a little time following these before embarking on the edit of your footage, the whole process should not take longer than a couple of hours. As with all things, a little practice and familiarity will allow this to become second nature, and dramatically reduce the time taken in future.

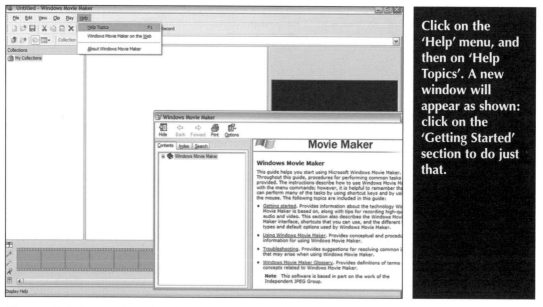

Figure 5.1 Accessing the video editing tutorial in MS Windows XP

Once you have captured and edited the video, it is useful to save each pupil's relevant footage as a different clip (you could use their name as the filename). If these are stored digitally (i.e. saved onto the network or computer's hard disk), they can then be used later on in the project in the Multimedia CD-ROM. If you feel comfortable compiling these into a single video file as well, this will make the running of the session more simple. In either case, the software makes the output of the video to CD-ROM or VHS tape simple; again, follow the relevant instructions for your program.

If you have not used a DV camera to record your footage, this will need to be digitally *captured* on a suitably equipped computer before the editing process can take place. There are many packages available to do this, and a full guide is beyond the scope of this book. However, again this is much less daunting than it may at first seem, and your specialist centre contact should be able to help you with this.

Running the session

To reiterate, the primary objective for the session is for pupils to gain an understanding that they are watching previously recorded footage, as opposed to live images, and that this footage has been stored on a computer, or on VHS tape.

In addition to observing and assessing pupils' responses to the video as it happens, it is also very useful to have a video record of pupil responses for review and assessment at a later date. However, if the pupils see themselves being videoed again, this may well lead to confusion about live and recorded images, as they will have associated the video camera with the live images in the previous session. To this end, it is a good idea to set up the camera (in a discreet place) before the pupils arrive in the teaching area, and have it recording, so as not to have to draw attention to it at any point during the session.

Although you could play the footage back to the pupils via a television, the impact is far greater if, again, you can project the images onto a large screen.

Hints and tips

- Play the footage of each child twice. After the first viewing, rewind and pause the video at a point where a good still image of the pupil is displayed. Ask pupils to comment on the differences between how the pupil looks on the screen and how they look at the moment. Play the clip through a second time. Use this to reinforce the idea that the footage has been recorded previously.
- Physically demonstrate (by showing/handing round) the medium (i.e. VHS tape or CD-ROM) on which the video is stored.

How to use a digital still camera

The purpose of this session is to allow pupils the opportunity to capture images which they feel are relevant to them, irrespective of their particular difficulties. The use of ICT here is to break down the physical barriers normally associated with this sort of activity. The pupils are also given the opportunity to learn that still images can be captured, stored and displayed in the same way that the video footage was in the last activities. Although this may seem like a retrospective step, i.e. intuitively we may think that the logical sequence would be from simple, still images to more complex, moving images, the process here is dependent on a greater degree of interactivity and input from the pupils themselves than in the last activities. The photographs taken during this session will also be included in the Multimedia CD-ROM.

Considerations

A good quality digital still camera is essential for this activity. Not only must it be capable of recording images onto some sort of removable media, e.g. smart card or floppy disk, but it must also be capable of outputting a live feed. Most digital video cameras available in the £300–500 range will be capable of both these. It is most likely that either the school or the specialist centre will already have a suitable camera available.

The output from the camera needs to be connected to the data projector, which will project onto a large screen. Again, as in the first activity, the large screen can then be used as a viewfinder for the camera, allowing the whole group to see what is being photographed, as well as those pupils who would otherwise have difficulty in using a small camera-mounted viewfinder.

The camera also needs to be mounted on a good-quality tripod, with a pan/tilt handle; this allows easy manipulation and lining up of shots for pupils with poor motor skills. Another desirable facility on the chosen camera is for some sort of remote shutter function. This is not often a feature of digital cameras, but it does enhance the ability of a pupil with poor motor skills to access the activity.

Carrying out the activity

The activity consists of two parts: pupils taking photographs of other pupils and teachers; and taking photographs of objects which are relevant to them. Pupils with poor motor skills will benefit most if they are presented with a range of relevant smaller objects to photograph, so that they can select those which are most relevant to them. These may include objects and equipment used previously as part of the course, i.e. DV camera, data projector, computer etc. In this way, they will be able to take photographs of a variety of objects, while still being able to use the large screen as a viewfinder.

Ask each pupil in turn of whom they would like to take photographs. When they have decided on their subjects, the selected people will need to be positioned in a chair for the photographs to be taken. Allow pupils to line the shots up themselves, while looking at the large screen as a guide. Try to get them to consider if the shot will have the whole of the person/object in properly, or if they just want to take a close-up of the face. Invite the rest of the group to comment on the composition of the shots (they, too, will be able to see this on the large screen). By using the tripod and a remote shutter switch, even those pupils with poor motor skills can arrive independently at a photograph of their choice and capture the image.

Allow each pupil to take several different shots of each subject; the selection of suitable images from this range will form part of the next activity. Those pupils able to operate the camera without the aid of a tripod and screen can go on to take photographs of other objects of their choice, without having to use the large screen or shutter trigger.

Hints and tips

- Make sure that you have a supply of back-up batteries for your digital camera. Using the external viewfinder can drain them very quickly.
- If you are using a camera which takes photographs directly onto floppy disk, make sure that you have a good supply of these also; one for each pupil is a good idea.
- Try to take images at the best-quality setting the camera will allow; file sizes can always be reduced later.
- Always try to involve the whole group in the process of lining up shots; this will greatly increase group interaction and often results in better images.

How to review, select and print images

The purpose of this activity is to:

- allow pupils to gain an understanding that images can be captured, stored, and displayed in a variety of ways;
- allow pupils to make judgements about the images that they took in the last activity; and
- select suitable images for inclusion in the Multimedia CD-ROM and the presentation for Unit 3.

To run this activity most effectively, you will need to use a teaching area which will allow you access to a data projector attached to a computer, a printer (preferably colour, and where possible, this should be directly connected to the computer, rather than a networked printer) and the media (smart card, floppy disk etc.) from the last activity which contains the photographs that the pupils took.

Demonstrate to the pupils, by taking the media from the camera, that the images which they took are now stored on that media. Ask them how you can show this. From here you can proceed by inserting the media into the computer (either in the floppy disk drive, or a suitable card reader) and browsing the images in turn. This can either be done from the explorer facilities in the computer's operating system (i.e. Windows or Mac Explorer) and this can then be projected onto the screen. It is worth pointing out here that the images are stored on the media, the computer is 'reading' them, and the projector is displaying them on the screen for the pupils to see.

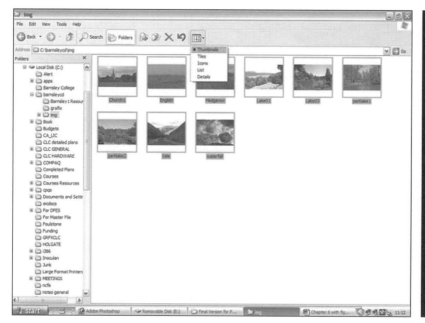

The button which is being selected here is the 'Views' button. Selecting 'Thumbnails' from its drop-down menu will show a small version of each image in that folder, as well as its file name. This makes reviewing and sorting images much more easy.

Figure 5.2 Browsing images in Windows Explorer

Hopefully, each pupil will have taken a variety of images of each different person/object, and you can involve the group by asking them which ones are the best, and why. When the pupils have expressed a preference for an image, demonstrate that the printer is attached to the computer by a cable. Print off the image, and point out to them that the computer is now 'sending the picture' to the printer, which prints it onto the paper.

By repeating this process for all the images you can reinforce the concepts that the images have been stored, and can be outputted in a variety of ways. By physically demonstrating the connections between the devices in this way, the ideas about where the information travels to and from are more easily understood by the pupils.

A short reinforcement sequencing activity can also be carried out, using photographs similar to the ones below. If these are cut out, the pupils can be asked to put them in the order in which they occur. After you have completed this activity with the pupils, you will need to copy the images which were selected to a separate folder for each pupil. These will be used in both the Unit 3 presentation, and in the final Multimedia CD-ROM.

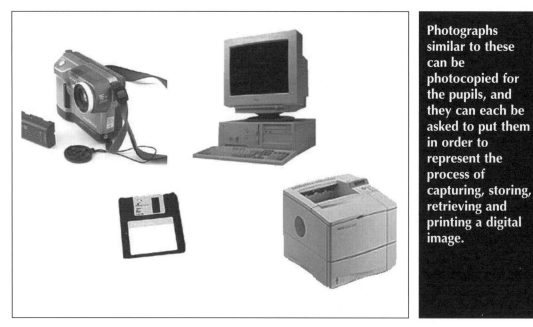

Photographs similar to these can be photocopied for the pupils, and they can each be asked to put them in order to represent the process of capturing, storing, retrieving and printing a digital image.

Figure 5.3 Sample photographs for sequencing activity

Hints and tips

- If you have pupils who find it difficult to express a preference for a particular image in this way, or need more intensive support, you could print off all the images relevant to the particular pupil, and allow them to select their preferred ones from hard copy; in some cases you will need to interpret their responses to each image in turn.

How to use a sound-maker

There are many different devices available today which have the ability to modify, or morph, sounds, usually aimed at the music production market. Perhaps more useful to this project are the family of technologies which actually produce or synthesise musical sounds, and are controlled by the user making bodily movements, seemingly in 'mid-air'. These devices use invisible, ultrasonic pulses to detect movement around their sensors, sometimes up to a distance of a few metres, and turn them into sounds which can be played through an amplifier or a PC.

These technologies have a real and pertinent application in the engagement and learning of children with learning difficulties, especially in removing barriers to learning due to physical difficulties. Because there is no need for a physical interaction, any part of the body can be used to produce sound; indeed, for pupils with little or no mobility, pushing a wheelchair through the sensor beams can produce a wide variety of sounds.

The purpose of the session is:

- to give the pupils the opportunity to understand that sounds can be produced and manipulated electronically;
- to enable pupils to understand that prerecorded sounds can be altered; and
- to allow pupils to make judgements about the quality and 'feel' of a variety of sounds.

Considerations

There is a fairly wide range of products available which will suit the purpose of the session. Ideally, the equipment chosen will allow the user to interact at a fairly wide range (e.g. over a metre), will be capable of producing a wide variety of sounds and will also have the ability to change sounds which are played through it.

Running the session

A successful session will allow all pupils to explore the possibilities of the sound-maker, and also encourage interpersonal interaction and co-operative working. As well as simply allowing the pupils to 'play' with sounds, there should be a structure to the session which encourages them to make judgements about the sounds being made.

Start off by demonstrating how the machine works; this is a good opportunity to physically show the arrangement of wires to and from the sound changer (see 'Equipment set-up' below) and to illustrate the concept that the machine itself is electronically producing sounds, and passing the sound information along the cables to an amplifier, which makes the sound louder (to varying degrees), and this information is then sent along more cable to speakers which turn the information into sounds that can be heard. Change the volume on the amplifier to show that this is the 'job' which the amplifier is carrying out.

Demonstrate a few of the different sounds that the machine can produce, and ask the pupils if they can think of words to describe them, or in the case of children with more severe difficulties, if they can indicate if they like them or not. Here you are introducing judgements about the quality and feel of the various sounds.

Allow each pupil in turn to explore making a variety of sounds, and ask for reactions from the rest of the group. Try to impress on them the need for silence when someone else is 'performing' and the need to listen carefully. The sound machines can usually be mounted on an armature similar to those used to mount switches; this facilitates the equipment being set up in a way which allows each pupil to use the most mobile part of their body to interact with the machine.

After each pupil has tried sound synthesis, play a song or piece of music with which they will be familiar. After you have listened it through once, play it through the sound-maker, but select one of the sound-maker's effects functions. Now any movement in the machine's sensor range will alter the qualities of the original track. Allow the pupils to experiment with this, and demonstrate the concept that sound information is being sent from the CD player or tape deck along cables; that the machine is now *altering* the sound electronically and sending the altered information to the amplifier, as before.

Equipment set-up

The equipment for this session needs to be set up as in the diagram below. It is worthwhile having all the cables used to connect the components visible, as this will allow easy demonstration of where the sound information travels from and to. Note that the second part of the session involves adding a tape or CD deck to the set-up. Try to do this only when you reach this stage. This will make it easier for the pupils to understand the functions of all the devices involved in a logical manner.

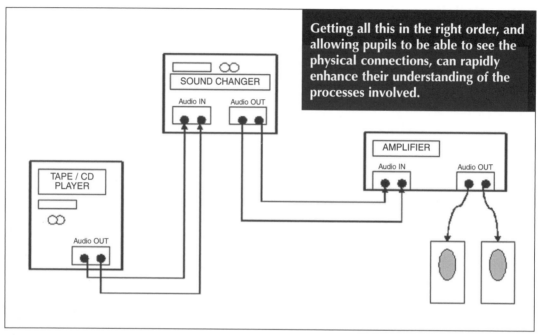

Figure 5.4 Setting up the sound-changing equipment

Hints and tips

It is always a good idea to spend some time before the session investigating the different effects and sounds available on your device. Try to select a range of different sounds that the pupils may react differently to, and be aware that some of the altering effects are for professionals wishing to improve sound quality, and may be too subtle for pupils to pick up on. In addition, be aware that some sounds may be startling to some pupils, and some may require more rapid and precise movements than others; these may be too inaccessible for some pupils.

How to capture sounds

In this session the pupils will revisit the sound-making equipment and record some of their preferred sounds, both from the sound-maker, and from other sources, if available.

The purpose of the session is to:

- allow the pupils the opportunity to understand that sounds can be captured electronically and saved for later playback;
- allow pupils to make choices about what sorts of sounds they like; and

- generate sound resources for inclusion in both the Unit 3 presentation and the final Multimedia CD-ROM product.

Considerations

- Although it is, of course, possible to record sounds with a conventional microphone and tape deck (and this is still very much 'ICT'), it is far preferable in this case to record sounds directly into a computer, for several reasons. This will allow easy compilation of the Unit 3 electronic presentation and the Multimedia CD-ROM, will allow sounds to be modified electronically and will facilitate instant playback and review of recorded sounds.
- Both PC-based and Mac-based operating systems come complete with a simple sound-recording program 'built in'. However, these often have a short time limit on the length of recorded sound clips, and will only store the sounds at a low quality. It is far preferable, therefore, to use a proprietary sound-recording program. There are a wide variety of these available, and some are very complex, and expensive. Equally, there are a great number of inexpensive, user-friendly packages available; some are available for free download from the internet. Your specialist centre contact should be able to offer some help in this respect.

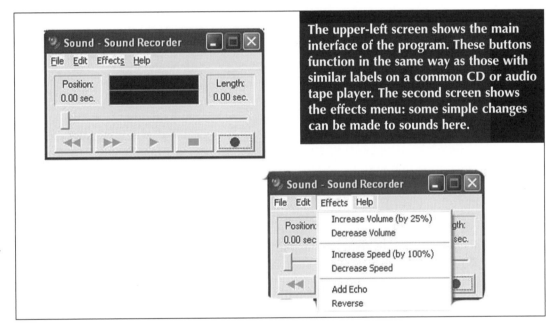

Figure 5.5 Windows XP sound-recording program

Running the session

The equipment should be set up in a similar way to the last session, but instead of the output from the sound-maker being plugged into an amplifier, plug it into the 'line in' socket on the soundcard of a PC. Also, be sure that the 'line in' input is selected on the PC for recording.

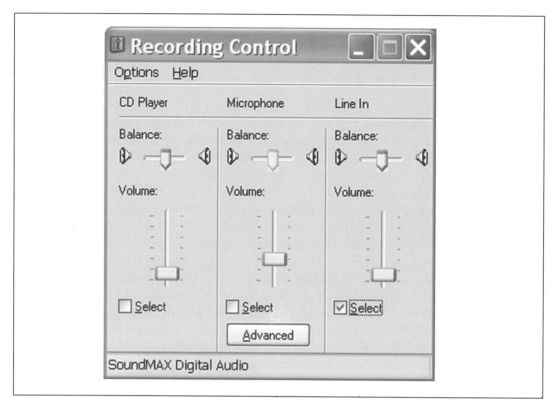

Figure 5.6 The recording control in MS Windows XP

The volume control is used to set the input level of the sound-maker or microphone (do not use the 'microphone' slider if you have the microphone plugged into the 'line in' socket). If the sounds that you are recording are either too quiet or too distorted, adjust the slider until they sound right. (It is a good idea to set this up before the start of the session.)

When you are ready, have each pupil come and record a few sounds each. Save each recording as a separate file (you could use the pupils' names as the first part of the filename followed by a number). This will make the compilation of the multimedia CD-ROM and the presentation easier later on.

Again, impress on the group the need to be quiet while another pupil is recording, and the need to listen carefully. After each pupil has recorded their sounds you can play the clips back to them and ask for their reactions. Make a note of the ones they like best; these will be used in the presentation.

Once the pupils have all recorded some sounds from the sound-maker, unplug it from the back of the computer. Take a microphone and plug this into the 'line in' socket instead. You are now ready to record other sounds made or chosen by the pupils. Demonstrate to them that the microphone is now attached, and try to get across the idea that the microphone is not making sounds but is capturing them, in a similar way to the digital camera capturing images.

Repeat the process of recording and storing files for each pupil, but allow them to speak into the microphone. If they are able, make some sounds with musical instruments, or record any other sounds that they feel are relevant to them.

Hints and tips

- Set the recording levels on the computer as described above, before the start of the session.
- Be aware that sound files can take up quite a lot of hard disk space. Make sure that the space is available on the computer that you will use.
- The better quality microphone that you use, the better the sound recordings will be. It is especially important for the group to be quiet and attentive when sounds are being recorded with the microphone, as this will also result in better quality recordings.
- If you have the time, it is worth spending part of another session reviewing the recorded sounds, and noting which the pupils react to best; these can then be used in the Unit 3 presentation.
- Five different sound clips for each pupil is about right for inclusion in the Multimedia CD-ROM.

How to manipulate sounds

This is one of the more difficult sessions to run, and one which will require help from your specialist centre contact. The activities involve altering the sounds captured in the previous session, and asking the pupils to respond and describe the changes that have been made.

The purpose of the session is:

- to reinforce the concepts that sounds can be recorded and stored for later use and that prerecorded sounds can be altered and saved in their modified form; and
- to allow pupils to make judgements about the quality and 'feel' of altered sounds, and about what alterations have been made to prerecorded sounds.

There are two broad ways in which this can be done:

Editing the sound files

There are many software packages available at low cost which will allow you to manipulate and change sound files. The complexity and capabilities of these vary widely, but most should have a few common functions.

Try changing the pitch of the recorded sound up or down, and then save the file. This can give particularly strange results when using recorded voice. Pupils can be asked if they can identify what the sound is, who it is that is speaking, and how the sound has changed (up or down).

Most packages will also allow you to reverse the sound file. Again, this can result in some strange sounds, and it is more difficult for pupils to guess what has been done to the altered sound by listening to it. However, by playing the original sound followed by the reversed sound a few times, some will gain an understanding of what changes have been made.

Other effects, such as reverb, can be added to the file, and pupils can be asked to describe how the sound is different. They will often come up with words to describe the effect, such as 'echoey'.

Using a software synthesiser

If you have more advanced equipment available to you, you may wish to try putting the original sound file through a software synthesiser. These software packages allow a midi-keyboard (akin to a piano keyboard, but linked to a computer) to be used to play back sounds when the keys are pressed. The pitch of the sound will be changed to match the pitch of the keyboard key pressed. This can be particularly effective with recorded voice. Again, pupils can be asked to comment on the sounds made, if they are at a higher or lower pitch than the original, and if their volume has been changed. The advantage of this method over the previous one is that the pupils themselves are far more involved in the playback of the sounds (via the keyboard which they themselves can operate), and may therefore engage more fully with the activity.

Hints and tips

- Use this session to revisit concepts covered earlier, such as volume and that sounds have been produced, recorded and saved for later use.
- Ensure that all pupils can hear the sounds adequately, by using amplified speakers, and arrange the room so that all the pupils can see each other. This will increase the possibilities for interaction, and responses may be improved.
- When changing the pitch of sounds, a shift of a half or a full octave is usually enough to produce interesting results. Any more than this will often make the sound unrecognisable, and the effect will have less impact.
- If using a keyboard and synthesiser to play back and change sounds, try to ensure that you have a long lead between it and the computer. This way you can involve every pupil in turn, without having to rearrange the seating.
- Save some of the modified sound files for inclusion in the final Multimedia CD-ROM product, as these are useful for revisiting work, and reflective sessions back at school.

How to set up and deliver the final presentation

This activity is not one in which pupils are directly involved, at least to start with. It involves the production of a digital slideshow of the work of each individual pupil, for presentation to an invited audience. The presentation is given as the final part of Unit 3: Communication.

While many teachers will be familiar with the sort of slideshow now commonly used in presentations, such as those produced in MS PowerPoint, some may not realise that the potential of these programs is much greater than simply to display text and graphics. The capability to play digital sounds and to display full digital video is a standard, but not often used, feature of these programs.

The presentation which is to be given by each child is easy enough to compile, and the expertise of the specialist centre contact will come in very useful here, but it is also useful to keep the following in mind:

- The pupils will be advancing the slideshow using a single switch, so ensure that all slide transitions or video play events are set to be triggered by the left mouse button only. The action of the switch emulates the left mouse button action in this type of program, so any other sort of control will be unavailable to the pupil, reducing their opportunities to deliver the presentation independently, and without intervention.

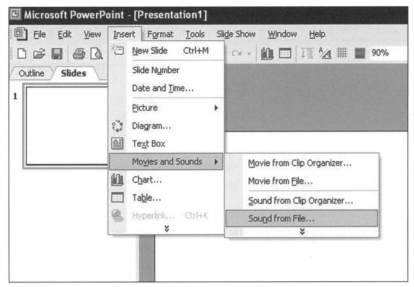

Figure 5.7 Inserting a sound into MS PowerPoint

- Use very few words on the slides: the audience wishes to see the pupils' own work, not a show made by the staff. Usually, a simple title, such as 'My Video Clip' or 'My Favourite Sound' is sufficient.
- Do not put any automatically timed events into the presentation. It is difficult to predict how quickly a particular pupil will be able to advance a presentation, and it may cause difficulties if the presentation was set to play something at an inappropriate time.
- While you may have a wealth of material available for each child, be sure to use only the samples that the pupils themselves have selected. This gives them an increased sense of ownership of, and pride in, their work.
- Keep the overall presentation length down to around four minutes maximum. This is a long time for pupils to be in front of an audience, and if there are several pupils in their group, the audience may also start to lose concentration.

Delivering the presentation

The presentation, once constructed, should allow each pupil to advance their own slideshow by using a simple switch and switch box attached to the computer. Make sure that the switch is set to emulate left mouse button action. Arrange the room so that the pupils can be at the front of the audience, but can also see the screen on which their presentation is being projected. This may mean using extension cabling to the switch, so ensure that this is all done safely and is affixed to the floor so as to avoid accidents.

How to compile the reference CD-ROM

This is the part of the scheme which is probably most open to individual customisation. It is important that the work done in this scheme, and the resources generated during it, are put to good use later on, and not just lost. The reinforcement of the learning and skills acquired here is vital, and this is made far easier if a digital resource is available for each child for later reference.

Essentially, the CD-ROM comprises all the digital resources: video, still image, sound, and final presentation, stored on a single disk. However, this can be further improved by creating some sort of interface for the contents of the CD-ROM; in other words making it interactive and easily used by both pupils and their parents, carers and teachers. This can be done in several different ways, but all will require some additional software, and a little expertise. The CD could be designed as a web page, able to be viewed on any computer, or another more specialist package for creating multimedia applications may be used. This is a stage which, again, will involve the expertise and resources available at your specialist centre. However, once the solution has been arrived at, future CD-ROMs for other classes will be easier to produce, and the teachers involved in the project will also have acquired the necessary skills and expertise to create them themselves.

In addition to the digital CD-ROM, you may also find it useful to have a series of the still images taken by the pupils printed out. These are best printed onto A3 paper, and then laminated and bound, so that each pupil has a portfolio of photographs which they themselves took. Again, these can be used to form the basis of future learning experiences.

CHAPTER SIX

Case Study – Fairview School programme

Fairview is a generic special school, catering for pupils with a wide range of special needs. As the programme is designed to be individualised for the needs of each pupil, the major difficulty for the school was choosing a small group from their Key Stage 4 classes. Whatever their level of need, all the pupils who were chosen benefited from the whole experience. This included being part of a group, sharing equipment, using unfamiliar surroundings and coping with working with a number of adults.

Inclusion has so many definitions, such as 'educated in the least restrictive environment possible' (Education Leeds 2000), that it is frequently denied to those pupils with the most severe and profound learning difficulties (often including gross and fine motor difficulties and sensory impairment). A question asked initially by staff from the special school was, 'How can mainstream facilities provide a suitable learning environment for these pupils?' One generally quoted response to these doubts is from the 'Ten Reasons for Inclusion' (CSIE 2000 www.csie.com): 'There is nothing going on in special schools that cannot also happen in a mainstream school, or is indeed happening somewhere.'

The National Curriculum does not acknowledge in its inclusion statement the need for a visionary approach, but it does state that flexibility in approach is vital for the success of inclusion for pupils with special educational needs:

> Teachers should take specific action to respond to pupils' diverse needs by (a) creating effective learning environments (National Curriculum 2000).

Implicit within this is the suggestion that attitudes and ethos of practitioners and institutions are the important factors for inclusion to be successful. All problems remain challenges or issues to be overcome, rather than insurmountable obstacles. It is reliant on the parents, staff, governors, head teachers and officers of the authority bringing their own desire for its success to the project.

The all-important extra funding came as the result of a successful bid from the local authority and it provided the teacher and support staff from the school. The Advanced Skills Teacher Scheme provides 20 per cent of the teaching time each week to outreach. This gave necessary time for planning, bringing staff together, and developing professional relationships in order to use staff as a team. It also gave valuable support in bringing out staff from the school. Our initial thought of using the programme as an opportunity for training in ICT access for support staff had to be pushed to a low priority at the first sign of resistance. The teacher was also available to work alongside the advanced skills teacher to plan the outline of the programme as it best suited the needs of the group. Meeting the needs of the individuals developed as the programme progressed. The beauty of the outline plan was the ease with which it could be adapted to suit the needs of a generic special needs group.

The programme was presented to staff in a way that demanded high expectations of the pupils and how this would be increased by combining the skills of both teachers and developing their different roles on the programme. The success of the programme for these pupils was, again, the willingness of staff to accept changes in working practices and to look for where we could access the same technology facilities and opportunities as all other school communities. Some of the support assistants who were not included in the planning of the programme doubted the relevance of the tasks and challenges set for the pupils. Could this have been caused by their own anxieties at being asked to work away from the small and familiar environment of the special school? Would this be an issue in need of addressing for others attempting to use inclusive settings? It was apparent that the school staff needed defined roles within the programme in supporting the pupils' welfare.

The staff of the Centre also had a problem, initially, in accepting both the behaviour of the pupils when moving around the Centre, and the positive behaviour management used by the AST and the support teacher from the school. A short familiarisation session with the staff prevented any clash of interests between the different approaches and different behaviours of the members of the community using the Centre.

This exciting programme of work had to be regarded as a whole-school project, involving staff back at base as well as when on the premises, and a whole-Centre programme in order that responses to pupils from staff were appropriate. Also, that the efforts of individual members of the Centre staff directly involved with the pupils was sufficiently valued by others; again, the small number of pupils created a false impression of the amount of work necessary by all involved for those more used to working with large groups of mainstream clients.

Delivery of the programme

When the pupils arrive in the school minibus, there is already a calm but busy atmosphere with groups and individual pupils working in the Centre. They are following different projects with teachers from mainstream schools in the area. That the pupils from the special school are among these other groups from the community of schools is an important factor in developing inclusive programmes of learning. Not every inclusive lesson involves everyone learning or experiencing the same programme at the same time, but being a part of the school community using a shared facility with each group challenged by their own programme fulfils the broader concept of inclusion as an educational and social concern. That the pupils are learning alongside others using the latest technology enhances the perception of the breadth of both the capability for learning and the creativity of teaching pupils within the special school range of needs.

Setting successful learning conditions and including those with highly complex needs values the response of all staff in meeting the needs of all pupils.

One of the main priorities when working with the Fairview group was to use the same advanced technology equipment for the group, but by differentiating the expected outcomes and diversifying the facilities and resources available, the team could ensure that each pupil would be sufficiently engaged and motivated by the tasks to accept and achieve the challenges set. Following the broad outline of the original programme, the team looked at the particular needs of the group and decided the format of the programme.

Within the Digital Imagery unit of work, the Fairview group took part in the following activities:

(a) video-conferencing from the City Learning Centre to classmates in school, including their class teacher;

(b) making video of selves working on-screen at tasks suitable to level of ability and needs;

(c) watching self on video;

(d) taking digital photographic stills of equipment, each other and staff involved (not an activity for PMLD pupils, although they accessed the stills on the large screen for choosing as part of their presentation);

(e) identifying favourite photographs of self or ones they were responsible for taking and printing; and

(f) looking at still photographs on large screen for group decisions.

This shows some changes to the original programme that reflect the different needs of the individual pupils in the group. The programme also showed some changes to the original programme in the Digital Sound Unit:

(a) accessing musical instruments including keyboards, drums and synthesisers;

(b) exploring different sounds produced by using the instruments alone or with a partner;

(c) using software that allows pupils to compose music by touching spaces on the smartboard; and

(d) exploring the use of the above, changing instrument sounds, tempo, musical styles etc.

The experiences of the pupils were then collated into a hard-copy book and an interactive CD-ROM as the pupils' own recording of the programme.

It is important to stress that this case study is intended to show how the same programme can be altered to meet different needs and also to extend teachers' development of the use and access of ICT. The similarities to the pilot programme will be obvious, but the differences will, hopefully, show that this programme is not designed to be set in stone, but to give teachers and others confidence to develop their skills, using the original programme as a framework within which to use their own creativity and desire to present their pupils of all different complexity of needs with a challenging but achievable programme of work. This enhances the valuable work within the special school, which tends to be limited in scope by lack of time, opportunity to work as a team of professionals and lack of access to the range of equipment and ways of making it accessible.

Following the programme as outlined above, the AST had the opportunity and the time, as part of the outreach element of her role, to evaluate the programme for each pupil and also to plot their achievements using the QCA Performance ('P') scales and National Curriculum targets depending on the levels of attainment of the individual pupils.

The following brief pen portrait of each pupil and their attainment levels at the end of the programme may give an evaluation of the possibilities this programme presents. Often, it is these descriptive and anecdotal studies of individual pupils that help teachers to make comparisons with pupils in their own schools.

All these pupils are in Key Stage 4 and from the full range of pupils at this generic special school.

Damian's profile

Damian is a capable pupil with moderate learning difficulties who lacks confidence in his abilities. While he is content to watch the adult model activities and new skills for him, he becomes very anxious when asked to take part. This is where the members of staff who know him well step in and use the strategies known to them to give him the necessary motivation and security to take part. He is computer-literate in that he uses ICT to find information, as a literacy and numeracy aid and as a word-processor. Following his excellent progress, Damian now has his own computer, with digital camera, at home. His parents are trying to access a photography course for him in his leisure time at a mainstream further education college.

Table 6.1 Outcomes for Damian

Activity	Comments	Attainment Level
Video	Gained confidence and able to verbally choose/negotiate. Spoke to the camera, rather than the adult, when responding to questions.	Level P8
Video-conferencing	Understood the interactive facility. He watched both settings on the screen and spoke to his class teacher and fellow pupils when shown on screen.	Level P8
Digital imagery	Learnt camera skills quickly. Exhibited a great interest in the use of the camera. Worked closely with the technician to print the photographs. Made considered judgements of the quality of the work he produced.	National Curriculum Level 2
Digital sound and sound production	Full use of drum kit, investigating sound properties using different actions and parts of the kit. Using visual software to produce sound, followed instructions closely, learnt how to use different elements of the programme. Could not manage to use the equipment without direct instruction.	National Curriculum Level 2
Celebration and communication	Chose own photos/video clips and sounds. Wrote script for presentation. Used staff for support when presenting his work.	Level P8

Adam's profile

Adam has learning difficulties and also his behaviour and learning styles are part of his Autistic Spectrum Disorder. His verbal skills consist of stereotyped responses and he has little spontaneous social speech. He has jerky movements and often will put his fingers to his ears or over his mouth when taking part in a group lesson. He finds the social rules of being part of a group difficult to adhere to and will often speak at inappropriate times or use language that does not fit into the situation he is in. He constantly looks to the adults he is familiar with from his own school. It takes him some time to settle into a different routine in a new situation, but he copes well. He is given the choice of joining in activities, often finding it easier to watch from the sidelines as others have a turn before having his turn. During his self-imposed observation times, he has learnt what is required of him, and so is confident to take part provided he is last in the group. He has some vocabulary that is not acceptable in social situations, although this is used only to shock and to divert attention from a situation he finds difficult.

Adam inspects each unfamiliar adult closely, noticing change in appearance from week to week. He needs to move around the room inspecting all the equipment, the doors and windows, switches and wires. When this is done, he feels able to settle and take part in the activities, initially as an observer. His support worker is unsettled about Adam exhibiting his less acceptable social vocabulary and actions and hinders his process of settling as part of the group by issuing instructions on his behaviour throughout the session. The support worker was moved to a different role when in the City Learning Centre, and Adam found it much easier to settle to tasks at his own pace and without the interruptions.

Table 6.2 Outcomes for Adam

Activity	Comments	Attainment Level
Video	Initial use of video was to shock staff with use of vocabulary and gestures. Soon settled and expressed his ideas and how he wanted to develop his actions and experiences.	National Curriculum Level 1
Video-conferencing	Understood the interactive nature of using video-conferencing. Gave information to his class teacher when he saw her on the screen. He also grasped that when he appeared on the inset screen, it was then his turn to speak/respond.	National Curriculum Level 1
Digital imagery	Adam assessed his use of the camera carefully. He was critical of his own perceived failures when he wasn't satisfied with the end result. He understood how to print the image from the printer, and also where it was stored.	National Curriculum Level 1
Digital and non-digital sound	Appeared to take his performance on the drums very seriously, repeating use of different parts until he achieved satisfactory sounds. Using software, he changed his compositions frequently, the number of choices making it hard for him to make a decision. Positive reinforcement from adults helped him to complete his tasks.	National Curriculum Level 1
Celebration and communication	Chose video clips, photos and sounds. He was very pleased with his presentation. As his work was shown it seemed to be an affirmation of the skills he had learnt and his increasing interest in the wider use of ICT.	National Curriculum Level 1

Dawn's profile

Dawn is an anxious pupil, who wants all her activities to be approved by adults. She goes from one to the other asking for reassurance. This anxiety was a barrier to Dawn forming relationships with the adults who were leading the programme and she constantly referred to her support worker from school. Breaking down this barrier required a level of co-operation that was difficult for her support worker to adhere to for long. Her protective nature towards her, in constantly reassuring her she was working well, seemed to exacerbate the situation and create an ever-widening gulf between the work she was presented with and her interacting with the equipment necessary to succeed. This issue emphasised the necessity of co-operation and of a lead adult to join the programme who has experience with pupils with complex needs and acknowledged expertise in this field. It required building the support worker's confidence in Dawn's abilities to interact with others and also benefit from the programme at her own level of ability and skill. As the programme progressed, the worker became more relaxed, and remained in an observation role rather than being a constant physical presence with Dawn.

Coming to a new situation, meeting new people and working on unfamiliar tasks with new equipment must have been extremely daunting for Dawn, more so than for the others in the group. One of our criteria for success with her was that she volunteered each week to come; the programme was not imposed on her from one week to the next. Following the primary anxieties and those of her support worker, she settled and grasped what was achievable.

Table 6.3 Outcomes for Dawn

Activity	Comments	Attainment Level
Video	Dawn responded to her moving image and that of the others in the room. She found it reassuring to name them as they appeared, and answered questions about them.	Level P6
Video-conferencing	'Students use ICT to interact with other pupils and adults' (QCA 2000c). Unsure of her role in interacting with the pupils at the other end of the video-conference screen. Found it difficult to grasp it was interactive and live. By the end of the session she did answer in single words with her class teacher.	Level P6
Digital imagery	Dawn used the camera to take photos and processed them with the printer and appropriate software with verbal guidance. '...save and retrieve simple information...' '...begin to choose appropriate pieces of equipment and software for an activity' (QCA 2000c).	Level P7
Digital and non-digital sound	Used drumkit, exploring making sounds using her feet and holding the sticks on both drums and cymbals, rather than banging them. She eye-pointed the equipment and stopped asking for constant approval for her actions; a great step forward. The screen composing was Dawn's favourite part of the programme, creating sounds and dancing to them when they were completed to her satisfaction. '...using their own initiative to exploit the potential of new ICT tools' (National Curriculum 2000)	National Curriculum Level 2
Celebration and communication	'Choosing digitised clips or photos...' (QCA 2000c) Chose her own photos and showed them to an audience with pride, using her work to illustrate her developing skills rather than verbal commentary.	Level P7

Richard's profile

Richard has very complex needs and would be described as being part of the group of special school pupils with profound and multiple learning difficulties. He has gross motor difficulties and needs a wheelchair for mobility. His fine motor skills are very limited and his reach and grasp are not fully developed. When he gets tired he loses head control and is subject to severe epilepsy with frequent episodes of absence. Due to his needs, the programme was modified for him, and we explored each area offered. As the original programme had been designed for pupils with profound and multiple learning difficulties, introducing Richard to the technology was exciting for the staff delivering the activities.

Richard's attention to task was limited, and his focus on the object of reference for an activity was very short. His limited use of reach and grasp had been sufficiently challenged by his school programmes within his usual routine, so important for pupils with this level of difficulty. However, coming to the City Learning Centre with his group was very different for Richard, as the other pupils were not taught in the same class as him during their time in school and so were virtual strangers.

As the adults working with Richard used the accepted early communication skills of eye contact and approaching on his own eye-level, he would reward them with a change in facial expression, sitting slightly higher in his chair, and occasionally a smile. Once all the adults working with him understood his responses to the stimulus presented, it was much easier for everyone to gauge the level of experience that was a suitable challenge for him.

Table 6.4 Outcomes for Richard

Activity	Comments	Attainment Level
Video	Responded to image of self on large screen. He imitated some of the actions he made on screen, which was accepted as an indication that he understood it was him. He was given the opportunity to... 'explore different sources of stimuli and information...helped to use information to make choices and simple decisions...' (QCA 2000c).	Level P2(ii)
Video-conferencing	Recognised familiar people on screen and by sound. His centre of focus returned to the screen repeatedly. Made sounds and looked towards the screen. 'Students begin to be proactive in their interactions' (QCA 2000c).	Level P2(ii)
Digital imagery	'...they begin to show interest in people, events and objects' (QCA 2000c). Richard showed interest using his own communication in his own still image on large screen and in that of others. Photographs of normal size were not appropriate to use.	Level P2(i)

Table 6.4 Outcomes for Richard (continued)

Activity	Comments	Attainment Level
Non-digital sound	'…perform actions by trial and improvement and remember responses over a short period of time'. Richard used drum-and-cymbal kit to produce sounds with both physical and verbal prompts. He held the sticks lightly and responded to the sounds he produced. He was aware of direct cause and effect. Looked to drumstick when it fell from his loose grasp. Used body movements and vocalising to communicate with adults his pleasure in his achievements.	Level P2(ii)
Digital sound	Using a synthesiser with sounds changing, dependent on movements Richard made with his hand. He very firmly communicated that he disliked the sounds and did not want to interact and produce the sounds himself, nor did he want the adult to do it.	Level P2(ii)
Communication and celebration	Single switch press to deliver presentation of his own image on video and still, showing him playing drums etc.	Level P2(ii)

The programme had been adapted to use different software, but the pupils who accessed it across a range of learning difficulties accessed the very latest in technology and met the challenges the whole project set them.

It is sometimes difficult to persuade staff from special schools that facilities are suitable for their pupils. However adaptable and creative teachers are within their own surroundings, using information technology can be a challenge that they may be reluctant to grasp as an opportunity for their pupils and themselves. Having good support strategies in place, in terms of the personnel delivering the programme, can encourage them to broaden the learning environment of their pupils and, at the same time, learn new skills that can be utilised in the future.

CHAPTER SEVEN

LEA-wide dissemination programme for Inclusive Multimedia ICT

It would have been easy to take our foot off the pedal, pat ourselves on the back and relax at the end of our inclusion project, Inclusive Multimedia ICT. After all, the project had been very successful; the pupils had made good progress; the partner school staff, parents and governors were positive about their involvement. The CLC staff were satisfied that the Centre had successfully included a group of youngsters and provided them with the chance to develop skills and resources for a wide range of learners. But we would have failed our students if we had relaxed. The whole point of the pilot was to start to develop a curriculum for pupils with the most severe learning needs in partnership with all schools with specialist provision. The hard work was yet to come.

At the end of the third unit, 'Digital Communication', the students gave a multimedia presentation to parents and carers, governors, school staff and some pupils. We had always intended to repeat the units with another class, so some of the pupils came along to see the kind of work in which they would be involved. But if we were to take our project wider than the one partner school, we knew it was important to invite a much wider range of representatives from other interest groups who would be able to witness what had been achieved; speak to school staff first hand; see the pupils demonstrating their newly found skills (and in some cases, confidence); make their own judgements about the effectiveness of the project; and thus speak with personal knowledge about our work from an objective standpoint. To this end, we invited representatives from the local education authority, including the Chief Education Officer, staff from special services and inclusion officers; a range of staff from other special schools and those with designated provision; and the press.

We went through a thorough evaluation process, taking on board all the comments and expressions of interest from our various presentation delegates and those involved in the project. Our evaluation took us in two directions: one route led to our development of the City Learning Centre curriculum and resources to meet the learning needs of pupils with a wider range of learning needs; the second route led to the production of an action plan to roll out our project to involve all special schools and designated service provision in projects across all the City Learning Centres (one already built, another two on the way) over the following three years.

The curriculum development plan for pupils with the full range of learning needs is covered in detail in Chapter 4. To roll our programme out we would need to bring together evidence of our work in order to persuade others to be involved. We intended to follow our project planning model as outlined in Chapter 2. Our potential new partners were not too far away. They were the other special schools, schools with designated service provision and the City Learning Centres. New project teams would be developed drawing on staff with existing relationships or bringing together new groups. The teacher adviser for inclusion was to play a key role in leading these groups and helping them to work productively together. The project teams would draw up their own project plans – not necessarily identical to ours, but benefiting from our experiences, curriculum development and evaluation outcomes. Although all the City Learning Centres were equipped to a similar level, each focused on slightly different specialisms, bringing further potential variety to the curriculum to be offered.

So we wrote an action plan. We worked closely with the inclusion officer from the LEA (we had made early contact with her when we were drawing up the guest list for the presentation event). She was now extremely helpful by putting us in touch with individuals who would be able to determine whether a potential roll-out would contribute to LEA priorities and in identifying sources of funding. The plan took the form of a proposal for extending the pilot inclusion project to pupils with PMLD, SLD and MLD in special schools and mainstream settings, initially taking place in the same City Learning Centre. As the remaining City Learning Centres came on stream, it was intended that the facilities they offered would be used to support inclusion across all the areas they served.

The action plan was written at two levels, mainly because we were unsure about the amount of funding we would secure. The basic action plan outlined a strategy that could be delivered over five years – a gradual roll-out to extend the curriculum we offered from that suitable for pupils with PMLD to one for pupils with SLD, and on to one for pupils with MLD and EBD, involving more City Learning Centres as the years progressed. The enhanced action plan got more schools and City Learning Centres involved earlier. We decided to aim high and wrote the plan as a roll-out over three years, with the five-year model as our safety net.

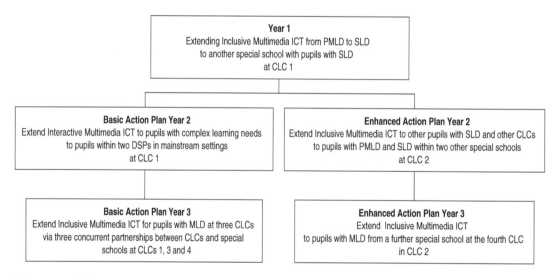

Figure 7.1 Overview of action plan to roll out Inclusive Multimedia ICT

Year 1

Working in our City Learning Centre, we would continue our work with the pilot partner school and deliver the project to another Key Stage 4 class of students with PMLD. At the same time, we would invite another special school, this time with students with SLD, to form a partnership. The original project team would be enhanced by a member of staff from the new special school and together we would modify our curriculum and resources to suit the learning needs of the new group of youngsters.

Year 2

Project A: following an evaluation of the curriculum experience for pupils with PMLD and SLD, Year 2 would focus on further planning to adapt Interactive Multimedia ICT for pupils within designated service provision in mainstream schools.

Project B: running alongside this, we intended to extend Interactive Multimedia ICT to the other City Learning Centres. One centre was already built and the third was due for completion by this time, so we sought funding to run programmes for students with PMLD and SLD with two other special schools in different areas of the city. The expertise gathered by the advanced skills teacher would be put to good use as she would advise, train, plan the curriculum and support the teachers and City Learning Centre staff involved in this next phase. If we had not secured enough funding, this project would have been programmed in for Year 3.

Year 3

By the third year of the project, we hoped that all the City Learning Centres would be involved in Interactive Multimedia ICT. Three would be involved in running projects for pupils with MLD if the funding was limited, the fourth being involved if enough was secured.

The action plan we submitted was successful, and funded to the level we had hoped. But in order to gain that funding we had to cost it clearly, and indicate how the completion of activities would be monitored and effectiveness evaluated against quantitative and qualitative success indicators. We had to be realistic, particularly with the time available from the advanced skills teacher for inclusion who only had one day per week to devote to this work. We also knew that we would need to secure time and commitment from the other City Learning Centre managers and special school head teachers.

The action plan could be presented to the LEA as being based on a successful pilot project in which pupils explored digital imagery, digital sound and communication skills. Those reading it knew that the students had used an impressive range of technology including digital still and video cameras, computers, music synthesisers, music software, musical instruments, interactive whiteboards and the conference facilities over a two-term period, because they had seen it themselves. There was nothing more persuasive for us than getting the right people in the right place to witness the pupils' achievements for themselves – that way, no one was in any doubt that the pilot had worked. We put a lot of effort into ensuring that the achievements of our youngsters were recognised beyond the City Learning Centre and the school. The pilot culminated in a presentation of work to parents/carers, other pupils and friends, staff from the partnership schools, representatives from the local authority and local councillors. It paid off then, and it continues to pay off as the action plan is enacted. Future project groups witness the progress students make at first hand (do read our account of this in Chapter 6 – our students would rise to the opportunity to be 'stars for the day'!). Success had been further reinforced in positive features in the local press. Just in case this is not enough, we also provide key individuals with a copy of presentation materials on CD.[1] You might consider this overkill – you might consider that we could get away with less. In our view it is a worthwhile investment. And it is great fun.

1   Don't forget to follow local guidance on taking digital photographs of students and to ensure parents'/ carers' permission has been gained.

Table 7.1 An example of part of the action plan submitted for the roll-out of Interactive Multimedia ICT

PRIORITY:	To extend the KS4 ICT (SEN) programme for Interactive Multimedia ICT						
ACTIVITY 1:	To review and extend the programme beyond the Red Route (PMLD – SLD) at Fairview with KS4 pupils						
Action Required	**Timescale**	**Staff**	**Success Indicators**	**Monitoring**	**Evaluation**	**Resources**	**Finance**
1. Meeting with HT/staff to discuss and present outcomes of the project	Sept 2001	CLC 1[1] Penny Road[2] Accred Co-ord[3] Fairview	Video-conferencing of presentation to the pilot partner special school	Scrutiny of proposed schemes of work Observation of delivery of curriculum programme and judgement of quality of teaching and learning by CLC	Effective inclusion of pupils in a community learning setting alongside mainstream pupils	0.5 day meeting day support 0.5 day AST time	£80
2. Presentation to pupils and staff of Fairview by Penny Road	October 2001	CLC 1 Penny Road Accred Co-ord Fairview			Effectiveness of provision for	0.5 day pupils presentation at the CLC 1 0.5 day AST time school assistants	Transport only
3. Staff development and training	Oct – Dec 2001	CLC 1 Fairview Accred Co-ord	School staff confident to use ICT facilities for the programme. Staff aware of expected pupil progress and appropriate next steps for learning (based on P scales).	ICT manager from videoed material and live sessions	improving ICT standards of teaching and	0.5 day 0.5 day AST time 1 day supply	£160
4. Planning the programme for Fairview	Dec 2001	CLC 1 Fairview x2		Review of ICT provision/teaching opportunities in PR and FV	learning for pupils with SENs	2 x 0.5 day meetings 2.5 days supply	£400
5. Curriculum programme delivered involving Penny Road staff including AST, CLC 1 and Fairview staff	Jan 2002 – Sept 2002	CLC 1 Penny Road AST Fairview staff + ICT Co-ord	Trial Multimedia Big Books with a further group of students. Develop SoW to include pupils of a wider attainment range. Further develop ICT skills of PR AST and ICT co-ordinator at Fairview.	Above by Accred. Co-ord. and LCC SEN School Improvement Adviser during Sept 2001–Sept 2002	Individual pupil progress evaluated over duration of the project, against performance indicators (P scales) for ICT	28 x 0.5 day visits to the CLC, one with up to five pupils. Supply cover for assistant in school.	£450 driver £520 SNA CLC 1 no cost
6. Explore the possibility of linking work experience for SEN pupils with MMBB programme	summer term 2002	Accred Co-ord Liaise with other schools	Identify schools and appropriate pattern of work experience for SEN pupils to work at the DFC	Review of work experience offered and outcomes by school co-ord and CLC		Pupils and support staff where appropriate	

1. CLC 1 manager: Liz Singleton; CLC Teacher Adviser: Iain Ross
2. Penny Road advanced skills teacher: Liz Flavell
3. Accreditation Co-ordinator: June Wilson

PRIORITY: To extend the KS4 ICT (SEN) programme for Interactive Multimedia ICT

ACTIVITY 1: To review and extend the programme beyond the Red Route (PMLD – SLD) at Fairview with KS4 pupils

Action Required	Timescale	Staff	Success Indicators	Monitoring	Evaluation	Resources	Finance
7. Production of big books and CD-ROMS	July 2002	Fairview Friends and Family	Each pupil to get their own MM Big Book and CD. Copy of CD provided for each school.	Scrutiny of finished work by pupils by schools and CLCs		Printing and CD copying	£200 A3 books £40 CD prodn
8. Review of SoW and inclusion programme	Sept 2002	CLC 1 Penny Road Fairview Accred. Co-ord.	Scheme of work revised to produce a programme for use by other pupils with PMLD at CLCs and back in school. Contribute to LCC Inclusion Programme of learning opportunities. Raise quality of ICT provision and range of teaching in schools.	Scrutiny of proposed SoW programme for use by future schools		2 days for CLC 1 FV/PR staff AST	£640 supply cover
9. Explore appropriate means of accrediting pupils' work	Sept 2001/2	Accred. Co-ord.	Identify means and accreditation of 100% pupils' work by the end of the course	Proportion of pupils accredited determined by the school annually Scrutiny of proposed SoW programme for use by future schools and project teams prior to project starting.			

CHAPTER EIGHT

Planning your own inclusion project

This chapter focuses on helping you to think through the stages involved in setting up and carrying through a successful inclusion project. We have considered five stages in project development; how our principles guided our aims at each stage; the issues we faced; the solutions we found; and a summary to guide you. We have also listed a range of possible inclusion projects to get you thinking about different opportunities or starting points for working with a partner school.

The stages we have identified are:

1. Why get involved in an inclusion project?;
2. finding the right partners to work with;
3. building your team;
4. developing an inclusive curriculum programme; and
5. sharing your successes.

1. Why get involved in an inclusion project?

This book has focused on demonstrating how innovative uses of information technology, within an inclusive environment, enable youngsters, facing a wide range of learning obstacles and with multiple learning needs, to make improved progress in their learning. There is an increasing acceptance of the value of inclusion and the national push for more inclusive educational provision (DfES 2001a). We are sure that as you read about the innovative projects we started (they are still running – sometimes it is difficult to know when something is no longer a project!) you felt that tickle of inspiration to do something similar yourself. Every time we describe the many ways our work helped our pupils to learn we feel humbled. As teachers, we plan for learning, but it is only when we see it happen that we truly recognise the learning potential of our youngsters. As you read about David realising what it meant to 'keep his head up straight' when he saw himself on the video screen, Ria demanding that the video camera be moved so that she could see her new trainers on the screen or Annabel refusing to press the button to move on to the next stage in her presentation to parents and governors because she wanted to hear the guitar music she recorded within the digital sound unit, it must surely have moved you, and it did us, to do more for the youngsters in your care.

But in writing this, we recognise that you are probably thinking that it does not feel as simple to you as we may have made it sound. Looking back on the successful elements within a project brings with it the benefit of being able to diminish the problems that arose during it and you are probably wondering how on earth to get started. The last thing we want to do is overwhelm you. In reflecting on this project it becomes easier to identify the steps we took on the way, and we would like to share these with you.

The first principle to accept is that there will be hurdles and you will need to consider ways of overcoming them. Whether you work in a mainstream setting, a special school or have a broader inclusion role, you will need to make contact with project partners because you simply cannot do this alone. Despite personal commitment and good intentions, you will probably be asking yourself how you could enable such collaborative activities to take place. This chapter reviews the role of individual teachers, schools, specialist centres and LEAs in promoting collaborative, inclusive educational activities. It will help you plan an inclusion project by predicting some (we cannot promise all) of the hurdles and pitfalls and indicating ways in which they can be overcome.

SUMMARY 1

Recognise that you will need to plan your inclusion project, predict obstacles and plan how to overcome them.

---

2. Finding the right partners to work with

This is an opportune time to start discussing an inclusion project. Finding a suitable partner school or centre requires one group taking the initiative to either build on or develop links and start a dialogue about inclusion. This is typically most effective when informal links already exist and when head teachers talk directly with each other. If you are a head teacher, the first step is to pull together a team of your own school staff, drawing on expertise from the LEA if required. If you work within a school, put together a draft proposal, discuss it with your head teacher, and persuade her or him to consider it with the head teacher of a potential partner school. The moral and management support he or she provides will enable your project to happen. For example, you will need release time; additional staff, when organising taking pupils out of school or when involving pupils in mainstream lessons; and help with arranging events such as a celebration evening for parents and governors. It will be the partnership managers that you will turn to for support. Therefore it is crucial that each school involved in the project has its own team to help plan and carry out the inclusion work. This team needs to be in regular contact with the head teacher and should expect to have to provide updates on the project implementation. There is no doubt that you will need support from colleagues in your own school during the project, so be proactive, involve all the right people and spread your inclusive enthusiasm.

Finding a partner school is the next hurdle. Ideally, partner schools would be co-located on the same site, share a common ethos and be committed to inclusion. But you may not be situated close to a suitable partner – and a good relationship with a school is less limited by proximity than it is by shared commitment to inclusion work. And you will need commitment – it is doubtless harder to engage in an inclusion project than not to bother. Therefore, it is inevitably going to involve more work at a time when some schools are finding it hard just to keep up with changes presented nationally and locally. If you are not sure which schools to consider working with, head teachers, school advisers and SEN services are a good source of knowledge about others likely to be willing to get involved. Look at the possibility of links with established, successful institutions such as beacon schools, specialist schools or centres where there is an emphasis on inclusion activities with the community or other local schools. Your local authority may well have advanced skills teachers or leading teachers with an identified specialism in inclusion. Such schools and individuals would have a responsibility to be involved in inclusion work and will probably be eagerly seeking partners to work with.

Figure 8.1 Finding a suitable partner

Another source of information would be local authority inclusion or special educational needs team members – they will know where likely partners may be found. Avoid initiating a project with a school or centre focused on other areas of development or engaged in different major school improvement activities such as those derived from being judged to have serious weaknesses or to require special measures – they will probably have enough on their plates as it is. The right partner will have the priority of developing inclusion written large within school mission documentation, curriculum statement and school improvement plan. They will see inclusive education as being embedded within their own improvement strategy. Be courageous and rigorous in finding the partner school or centre with the right ethos and commitment.

If you have a good relationship with a local school, a partnership may be a natural development of this. Some schools belong to 'families' or 'pyramids', commonly grouped by feeder primary and receiver secondary school relationships. In some larger local educational authorities, schools are grouped into 'wedges' or 'areas'. Funding streams focused on education action zones, social regeneration or neighbourhood renewal provide a link between some schools, particularly those with common needs. It is much easier to work with existing structures, some of which engender common purpose linked to shared funding priorities and, for some, enhanced facilities such as City Learning Centres or family learning centres. Consider existing structures and relationships first when seeking a partner.

Finding a partner close to your own school or centre is an advantage for obvious reasons. It is easier to nip around the corner to plan learning or try out unfamiliar resources. Equally, it is not fair for youngsters to face unnecessarily long journeys – especially when many attending a special school may already have travelled some distance from home. Careful planning can minimise the downside of moving pupils around; for example, meeting pupils at the partner school or centre obviates the need for an additional journey. Also, the value of the journey can only be measured when we know how much pupils and staff can gain from being involved in the project. It is all part of the risk assessment and believing in the importance of taking time to find the right partners. Special schools may not always be located right next to mainstream schools – but, then again, they do have access to buses and, typically, a culture of taking pupils beyond the premises for learning. The journey is worth it if the learning opportunity provided is too. So don't be put off by distance – once the pupils are on the bus the length of the journey (within limits) to a good partner school or centre will be worthwhile.

Excellence in Cities, launched by the DfES in March 1999, provided an opportunity for inclusive working in the form of City Learning Centres, and reinforced the development of specialist schools. City Learning Centres (CLCs) are large ICT-packed centres with a mission for transforming opportunities for, and attitudes towards, learning (DfES 1997a). Many specialist schools, beacon schools and city technology colleges are committed to working on inclusion, and some specialise in the range of resources available. Look beyond your school to find institutions able to extend the range of resources and learning experiences for your pupils. For us, it was more than just the kit that made the CLC ideal for the project; it was also the ethos. We were determined that the project should feel like something very different from school learning. Pupils of all ages came to the CLC, as did adults on training courses from schools and local businesses. The environment provided was intentionally different from schools. Inclusion was the norm. Pupils and adults mixed in the cyber café, and the equipment provided was of commercial quality. Nothing was watered down. Our youngsters experienced using the same conference facilities as adults attending as course delegates. If you intend to form a partnership with a specialist centre, consider what its 'specialist' features are, including whether a truly inclusive ethos will be part-and-parcel of the project experience.

Schools and centres are not always easy to get to or around, and despite the best intentions of SENDA, some buildings are never going to be 100 per cent accessible. However, all public buildings, including schools, now have to have an accessibility plan and must be working towards making more learning areas available to all visitors regardless of disability. Building accessibility varies considerably. New buildings should be better – though practice tells us that wherever you take youngsters with differing degrees of mobility it is rare to find visits smooth and hassle-free. Depending on the needs of the included youngsters, a minimal requirement might well be access to a disabled toilet. There may be a need for a fully fitted hygiene suite, depending on the duration of the visit to the centre or partner school and how far the class have travelled to attend. In our case, although the hygiene suite was available in a school adjacent to the City Learning Centre if we needed it, we did not use it because the majority of pupils used the facilities we had, or were not with us long enough to require changing in the suite. Discuss the hygiene needs of the youngsters with partner schools, and don't over-complicate the requirements – you might find that access to specialist facilities is less of a problem than you might think.

It is important to visit potential partner sites and to encourage managers to be clear about both the limitations and potential of the site, in general and specific curriculum areas, for inclusion activity. And remember that you will not need to access every room in the building – just the ones with the learning facilities you require. When discussing an embryonic project consider which specialist facilities will really enhance learning for the youngsters, both in curricular and social terms

SUMMARY 2

Find the right partner. Ethos and commitment to inclusion is number one priority. You will also need to consider travel time, accessibility to the building itself, and the specific learning resources within. Consider using a specialist centre to enhance the facilities you may already have in school, though the centre must provide more than the kit – the atmosphere and ethos provided must be truly inclusive.

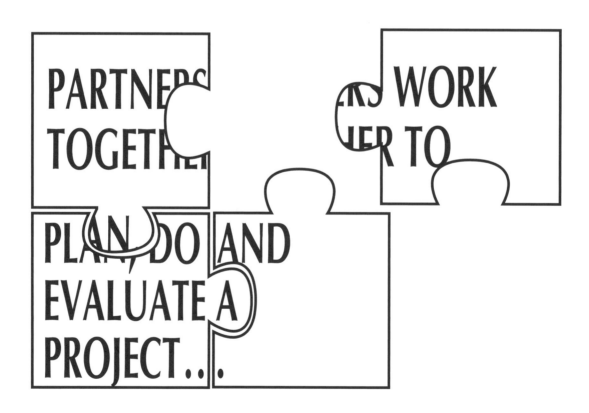

Figure 8.2

3. Building your team

Identify a small, cohesive planning team and use national best practice as the foundation for curriculum planning. Gain the commitment of your partners for a small-scale, focused pilot. Having secured the kit and the ethos, the next stage is to be clear what you want the pupils to achieve with it.

You will stand the best chance of achieving your goal of a successful inclusion project when you pull together a team with the combination of knowledge, understanding and skills, plus the ability to work collaboratively. Let's take a moment to reflect on what that meant to our project. We took time to identify what we meant by 'knowledge, understanding and skills' and to ensure that at least one person in the team already had them. But we did not want 'expert consultants' to swoop in, carry out specific tasks and then leave our team. What we sought were experts who were as willing to work collaboratively to impart their skills to others as they were to use them with our children. Members of the project team were then able to develop new skills and to further the project back at school or with other groups of children by either reinforcing activities with youngsters or passing skills on to other staff. Figure 8.3 shows the key roles played by members of the project team.

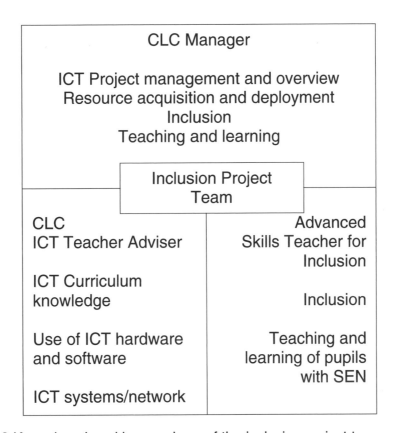

Figure 8.3 Key roles played by members of the inclusion project team

We established a planning team of three (more detail can be found in Chapter 3) and involved others with specific skills to support us. The project planning team consisted of the Centre manager, an advanced skills teacher from a local special school and an ICT advisory teacher who also worked at the City Learning Centre. Other staff who became involved in the project included the pupils' teacher and support staff from the special school. It is worth saying at this point that whatever we came to the project with, by the time it was finished we were all far richer for the experience. The City Learning Centre had 'learning at the heart of the community' as its motto, and we all considered ourselves to be learners.

Any good partnership requires commitment, and in our case, most of this manifested itself as release time for the Centre staff and advanced skills teacher – initially to meet to discuss common aims and determine the needs of individual pupils, and then to plan and deliver a substantial curriculum programme within an inclusive setting. We started small, with a pilot project involving one group of Key Stage 4 pupils. We focused on ensuring the curriculum programme placed an appropriate degree of learning demand on the youngsters. Not least, we met their needs rather than satisfied our urge to use amazing pieces of kit. We also explored the practicalities of allocating staff time, organising transport, involving parents and ICT resource requirements. Through the pilot we learnt what we needed to know in order to spread our vision wider.

There are many contexts in which pupils can access activities, and working with adults with a different experience of learning can stimulate creative ideas and approaches. Work collaboratively with your partners and bring in others with different ideas about learning and expertise in the field of inclusion. Use the skills of your partners, listen to each other's ideas and don't be afraid to try something new.

We found discussing our ideas with others beyond our project team extremely helpful. It clarified our thinking, and also started the process of spreading the word about what we were doing. Keeping an eye on the local and national agenda for inclusion was important in ensuring that we were on the right track in terms of curriculum planning and delivery.

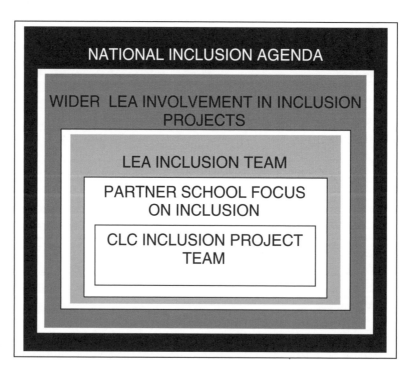

Figure 8.4 The place of our inclusion project in the developing local and national inclusion agenda

SUMMARY 3

Build a small core team with representatives from each of the partnership institutions. Don't be afraid to ask others with particular skills to join you. Draw on the expertise of others as you go along, seek out those who have gone before you, and make the most of existing good practice and practitioners.

4. Developing an inclusive curriculum programme

We are encouraged to be creative in education and to be moderate and measured risk-takers. In developing our inclusion project we took a risk when a special school teacher was inspired to bring a class of Year 10 students into the City Learning Centre for one half-day a week for a minimum of two terms, instead of leaving them to learn via the perfectly good curriculum within their own school. The risk was balanced by the inclusion project team who planned a curriculum experience based on guidance within the National Curriculum for Information and Communication Technology, supported by guidelines on 'Planning, Teaching and Assessing the Curriculum for Pupils with Learning Difficulties' (QCA 2001). National Curriculum 2000 provides a starting point for planning an inclusion project. Within the section 'Inclusion: providing opportunities for all children' teachers are charged with responsibility to provide 'suitable learning challenges', respond to 'pupils' diverse learning needs' and overcome 'potential barriers to learning and assessment for individuals and groups of pupils'. What this can mean in practice varies as much as our schools and the situations they find themselves in.

Using the Key Stage 4 ICT National Curriculum, we identified the need for pupils to learn about controlling devices; to locate pictures, sounds and other information; and to create a multimedia presentation. We focused on digital imagery using video and stills photography to provide a range of short, focused tasks such taking pictures, observing images on a large screen and choosing images to capture. Digital sound was an opportunity for pupils to generate a range of sounds using both instruments and sound-generating hardware, to listen to sounds and feel the vibrations associated with them; and to capture sounds. Digital communication provided pupils with the opportunity to use a range of control devices (mainly appropriate switches and links embedded into an electronic presentation) to communicate their work. National guidance helped us place CLC resources in a curriculum context by providing examples of how the principles of an appropriate KS4 curriculum for ICT can be applied. Translating principles into practice through exemplification is supportive as long as that fine distinction between advice and prescription is clearly maintained. As soon as documents are written to exemplify principles, it seems the end-product is then interpreted as limiting – even if that was never the intention. The interpretation we placed on the ICT curriculum (see Chapter 4) is not necessarily one for you to follow – quite the reverse. Using the programme of study merely gave us a starting point for identifying attainment-related learning objectives, and age-appropriate activities.

We have major changes in legislation to support greater inclusion. There is a national emphasis on promoting the inclusion of children with SEN within mainstream schools wherever possible. We have the expectations explicit within the National Curriculum. The impact these will have on the curriculum offered is in the hands of curriculum innovators, or in other words, it is down to us. Our book has exemplified creative interpretations of the National Curriculum by teachers in a particular situation. Take these in the spirit intended – as an example of what is possible within the umbrella of inclusion – not necessarily the only recipe to guaranteed success. When building your own inclusive curriculum, start with your children and staff and *their* learning needs.

> **SUMMARY 4**
>
> **The basic toolkit for developing an inclusive curriculum is there. It is up to us, the teaching and learning professionals, to use the tools creatively when planning inclusive learning opportunities.**

5. Sharing your successes

The successful projects documented within previous chapters started with a shared vision. Simply, we wanted to have a positive impact on the achievement of youngsters with learning needs ranging from the profound and multiple, through severe and moderate, to emotional and behavioural, by giving them access to the latest information and communications technology within an innovative, age-appropriate curriculum experience in an inclusive setting. This sounds like a tall order, but consider it as an adventure into the unknown. Like most adventures, the key is to work with others to plan ahead and the journey is more interesting when you take others with you in both body and spirit. If you are going to persuade others to come on board, it is important that you are all clear about the destination. You might not know exactly the path to be taken – indeed we would argue that you need to be prepared for all partners to influence the directions taken – but you must know why the journey is important and what it will contribute above and beyond the existing steady path your youngsters and colleagues would be following anyway.

Before you leap off to a blank action plan format (a tool now familiar to schools across the land), consider another basic principle: if something is worth developing, it is worth having a bash and doing it 'badly' rather than spending hours planning it and never doing it at all. Take time to clarify your reasons for, and expected outcomes of, an inclusion project; and start small. We did not know we were starting an 'inclusion project' when we began our work, and our initial plans were focused around just one group of pupils with profound and multiple learning needs. The staff at the City Learning Centre had a vision about the use of ICT to support learning, and knew a special school head teacher who was creative, innovative and prepared to take a risk in designing the curriculum she provided. Links were made with the special school, ideas were shared and a commitment to staff time and pupil involvement made. We shared this vision with like-minded others, and by agreeing to work collaboratively a partnership was formed with staff from a special school and a City Learning Centre.

In the first City Learning Centre inclusion project the class did not work with other students. However, they did mix with all Centre users in the cyber café and used impressive ICT kit such as digital video and stills cameras, interactive whiteboards, musical instruments and audio sound-generators. The digital presentation to parents, other pupils, governors and LEA representatives provided a unique opportunity to demonstrate their learning to others. As the project rolled out to others there was greater involvement of youngsters from different schools (you can read about these in Chapter 7).

Inclusion has many forms. It is not necessarily about placing youngsters with different learning needs in a class together. The broader your interpretation of 'inclusive activities that enable pupils to learn in different settings with age-appropriate activities', the greater the range of initial project ideas you can start off with.

There are other groups that are important partners in an inclusion project. A school is a community, and, as such, there are interrelationships to maintain in order for a healthy ethos to be sustainable. We must keep the bigger picture of creating an inclusive culture in clear focus when planning an inclusive activity (CSIE 2002). Students, staff, governors and communities beyond the school will need to be involved in partnership in different ways. Within an inclusive school, all staff will operate at their best when working collaboratively. That requires us to talk to colleagues about a proposed project, to invite involvement and to identify how the activities will contribute to learning for pupils, professional development for staff and the whole-school focus of establishing inclusive values. Parents entrust their children to us and are rightly unwilling for them to be used as guinea pigs. Parental permission is a must to take youngsters beyond school – but we want more than that; we also want their confidence and blessing. Governing bodies have a duty to ensure the school delivers a curriculum entitlement and appreciate being consulted and kept informed. Other teachers have a curriculum to deliver too, and we must avoid tensions caused by removing pupils from classes led by others without their agreement. Last, but not least, students have the right to expect that their learning is focused on developing the skills, knowledge and understanding that is appropriate for them. In order to enable an inclusion project to take place, it is inevitable there are other groups who need to be informed and involved at different levels. If you have a good idea, share it with others, involve a wide range of individuals and invite their further participation. If you fear being flooded with volunteers you must be onto a winner!

Remember, start small and have a bash; you can expand later. Communicate about the work you are planning, and involve others in establishing inclusive values.

SUMMARY 5

Contribute to the development of an inclusive culture by sharing your vision for the inclusion project with your school community and project partners. Be prepared to ask others what they think about your plans, how they felt about activities as they took place, and to reflect on whether it was worth doing and how it could be done better next time. Reflection and evaluation are key to maximising the effect of the work we do. Plan ahead to gather the photos, organise celebration events and distribute evaluation material to enable you to review effectively and disseminate what you have done so that others can benefit from it.

Some potential project ideas

- Bring pupils to a partner school for a specific social programme, e.g. for a weekly lunch, to see a production.
- Encourage youngsters from mainstream to work with pupils in the special school as part of a community placement, Duke of Edinburgh Award or other school initiative.

- Take youngsters from a partner school on a joint trip and allocate partners to each pupil from a special school. Include specific activities to encourage working together, e.g. visit to a theme park or amusement arcade, walk along a beach, rockpool hunt, visit to sea-life centre, visit to a bird garden or local site of natural interest.
- Partner youngsters of a similar age and encourage them to work together on a specific project, e.g. music or art production, development of a sensory garden.
- Offer a shared curriculum experience within which learning objectives may be very different, but activities may use the same equipment or similar experiences, e.g. food technology (making bread), science (environmental project), history (visit to Victorian school room or centre).

APPENDIX

Curriculum plans

Unit 1: Digital Imagery

ICT SEN KS4

ABOUT THE UNIT

This unit involves pupils and students in the capture and manipulation of both still and moving images. This includes moving images of themselves, plus images of familar objects and people relating to their personal life as well as the ICT curriculum.

This unit is divided into 4 sub-units:

1. Watching ourselves live

2. Watching recorded footage

3. Capturing still images

4. Using computer hardware to review, select and print digital images.

WHERE THE UNIT FITS IN

This unit allows children with special educational needs to access curriculum learning opportunities/experiences, not typically available within a school context, via the use of ICT. The scheme covers the ICT POS with regard to using switches to operate a range of computer hardware and capturing, storing and retrieving digital images.

This unit assumes that

- staff have access to technical equipment – typical of that found in a City Learning Centre
- staff have access to relevant software and expertise
- learning objectives for ICT and for other areas (e.g. motor/sensory skills) are included.

TECHNICAL VOCABULARY

- Image
- Camera
- Digital Video
- Projector
- Screen
- Computer
- Printer
- Floppy disk
- Memory card
- Tripod
- Capture
- Save
- Load

RESOURCES

- Digital still camera
- Digital video camera
- Digital video cassettes
- Video-editing software
- Batteries
- Data projector
- Screen
- Floppy disk
- Tripod
- Switches

EXPECTATIONS LINKED TO P LEVELS	
TOLERATE *(Encounter)*	Pupils are willing to be present during an experience or activity. For some pupils who may typically withhold their attention or presence from many situations, their willingness to tolerate, e.g. watching live footage of themselves, may in itself be significant.
REACT *(Awareness)*	Pupils react to moving or still images by changing their pattern of behaviour e.g. briefly react to a live or recorded image of themselves.
RESPOND *(Attention and* *response)*	Pupils change their body language, e.g. facial expression, as a result of a stimulus such as seeing a live or still image. Pupils may show delight, surprise or dissatisfaction as a response to the activity.
ENGAGE *(Engagement)*	Pupils make a more purposeful movement or show more consistent attention to events during the activity. They may watch photographs being taken or may interact with a live image of themselves on the screen.
ANTICIPATE *(participation)*	Pupils positively or negatively anticipate outcomes such as an image of themselves on a screen. They may show signs of excitement in their willingness to participate in the activity; for example, wanting to take a photograph or use a video camera. They may be reluctant to take part – indicating an understanding of what is likely to happen. Some staff encouragement may be involved.
CHOOSE *(involvement)*	Pupils choose to be involved in the activity or make choices during the activity. They may request stimulus, e.g. by pointing or looking at a piece of computer equipment to be photographed.
LINK EXPERIENCES *(gaining skills and* *understanding)*	Pupils make use of skills, knowledge, concepts or understanding from previous learning experiences. They recognise familiar images or equipment. They may know that a button needs to be pressed to capture an image.
Progression within Linking Experiences (moving from concrete through to more abstract application)	
P4 (concrete, repetition)	Pupils following step-by-step instructions to carry out a basic process, e.g. they will purposefully use a camera to capture an image.
P5 (link to model)	Pupils follow instructions involving more than one step at a time; for example, they capture an image using a digital camera following instructions. Pupils indicate changes, such as when watching recorded footage of themselves they realise they are wearing different clothing.
P6 (understand how to make changes)	Pupils observe changes within the video and make a connection between the image and themselves, e.g. pupils move their hands and feet to ensure they appear on the projected image on the screen.
P7 (apply to range of new situations)	Pupils look through a series of images and select a favourite one, e.g. to save or print.
P8 (apply sequentially with understanding)	Pupils know that images are stored and can be retrieved from a floppy disk. They respond to new terminology and can find objects when asked, e.g. will put a finger on the button or operate the printer when asked.

LEARNING OBJECTIVES	POSSIBLE TEACHING ACTIVITIES	LEARNING / EXPERIENCES	POINTS TO NOTE
PUPILS SHOULD LEARN / EXPERIENCE			
SUB-UNIT 1: WATCHING A LIVE VIDEO FEED **Setting the scene** The first session will last approximately two hours, or possibly more if there are a larger number of children in the group. It is important that: • all pupils are positioned appropriately to ensure they have a good view of the projected image. • individual pupils are positioned in front of the digital video camera when it is their opportunity to be filmed.			
• that a camera and projector can provide a live image of themselves • to gain a better understanding of their relationship to their surroundings • to interact with their own live moving image	• Using a digital video camera to project a live video feed onto a large screen • Move body parts to investigate the limits of a camera's field of vision • Compare moving the body and moving the camera	• A camera can capture moving images • The camera has a limited field of vision • Record footage for use in a later unit	• Moving the body changes the image displayed on the screen • Moving the camera changes the part of the room displayed on the screen • Movements in front of the camera should be either voluntary or prompted on the part of the pupil. In the case of pupils tolerating an experience the movement would be directed by a familiar adult.

LEARNING OBJECTIVES	POSSIBLE TEACHING ACTIVITIES	LEARNING / EXPERIENCES	POINTS TO NOTE
PUPILS SHOULD LEARN / EXPERIENCE			

SUB-UNIT 2: WATCHING RECORDED VIDEO FOOTAGE
Setting the scene

In this block, the pupils watch the video footage recorded in the last block on a large screen. Their reactions to this footage are videoed.

It is important that:

- each pupil's footage is played in turn and all pupils watch each section of footage.
- pupils are positioned appropriately so that they all have a good view of the screen.
- the camera being used to record their reactions is not visible to the pupils (this will avoid any confusion regarding live/recorded feeds).

LEARNING OBJECTIVES	POSSIBLE TEACHING ACTIVITIES	LEARNING / EXPERIENCES	POINTS TO NOTE
• that moving images can be stored and replayed at a later time • to discriminate between the image of themselves on a pre-recorded video and the way that they appear currently • to watch recorded footage of others	• Pupils watch pre-recorded footage of both themselves and others • Pupils indicate differences between their real time movements and the movements of themselves played back on the screen	• pupils recognise parts of their own body when their face is not visible on screen	• Reactions indicating an understanding of the differences between live and recorded images may need to be interpreted by a familiar adult. Discreetly videoing the response of a pupil will aid in assessing and recording this. • **Unit 3: Communication** will result in an interactive CD-ROM which can be used to support follow-up activity involving matching movement to recorded footage

LEARNING OBJECTIVES	POSSIBLE TEACHING ACTIVITIES	LEARNING / EXPERIENCES	POINTS TO NOTE
PUPILS SHOULD LEARN / EXPERIENCE			

SUB-UNIT 3: CAPTURING STILL IMAGES
Setting the scene

In this block, the pupils will focus on using a digital camera to record still images, making their own decisions as to what images are appropriate for capture.

It is important that:

- the output from a digital camera viewfinder is passed through to a data projector to allow pupils with poor gross motor skills to effectively line up shots, and to allow others to participate in the process

- a large tripod with a long handle is used to allow easy pan and tilt of the camera by pupils

- a large switch or shutter extension cable can be used initially to allow pupils to independently choose when to take the shot

- pupils are given the opportunity to respond to saved images, deciding on which ones will be used in the Unit 3: Communication sessions.

LEARNING OBJECTIVES	POSSIBLE TEACHING ACTIVITIES	LEARNING / EXPERIENCES	POINTS TO NOTE
- that a digital camera can capture and store images - to make decisions about which objects or people they would like to photograph - to review captured images on a screen - to independently compose and shoot their own photographs	- Pupils take it in turn to operate the camera; lining up shots of their chosen objects or people and deciding when to release the shutter - Pupils interact with each other and the pupil currently operating the camera to express positive or negative opinions on the composition of each shot - Pupils view stored images on the big screen and give reactions to them - Pupils' favourite images are stored for later use	- that a camera can store still images - that stored images can be reviewed later - that images can be projected onto a large screen - indicate a preference for particular images - controlled use of gross and fine motor skills to compose relevant shots	- Movements to compose shots should be either voluntary or prompted on the part of the pupil. In the case of pupils tolerating an experience the movement would be directed by a familiar adult. - **Unit 3: Communication** will result in an interactive CD-ROM which can be used to support follow-up activity involving reviewing, and expressing preferences for, pre-recorded still images.

LEARNING OBJECTIVES	POSSIBLE TEACHING ACTIVITIES	LEARNING / EXPERIENCES	POINTS TO NOTE
PUPILS SHOULD LEARN / EXPERIENCE			

SUB-UNIT 4: REVIEWING, SELECTING AND PRINTING STORED IMAGES
Setting the scene

In this block, the pupils will review the photographs which they took in the previous block, respond either positively or negatively to the images, and print hard copies of the images which they indicate as their favourites.

It is important that:

- pupils are positioned appropriately so that they all have a clear view of the screen
- each pupil's set of stored images are reviewed on a large screen by the group; responses are given for each
- images are displayed from a computer to which the images have been previously transferred, not the digital camera.

LEARNING OBJECTIVES	POSSIBLE TEACHING ACTIVITIES	LEARNING / EXPERIENCES	POINTS TO NOTE
• that images can be captured by a camera and stored for later use • to view stored images from a computer • to respond to, and express an opinion of still images • that images can be displayed on a screen, or printed onto paper • to use visual discrimination	• Pupils review and respond to images displayed from a computer, both of themselves and other pupils in the group • Pupils engage in the process of selecting their favourite images • Pupils take part in the process of printing off favourite stored images	• recognise that images have been captured and stored	• controlled use of fine motor skills to print still images • recognise that images have been stored on storage media (e.g. floppy disk) • recognise that images have been processed and displayed by the computer • recognise that images have been sent along a cable to a printer, which transfers them onto paper	• Reactions indicating a positive or negative response to images must be voluntary or prompted on the part of the pupil. A familiar adult may need to interpret these responses in the case of some pupils • **Unit 3: Communication** will result in an interactive CD-ROM which can be used to support follow-up activity involving reviewing, and expressing preferences for, pre-recorded still images.

Unit 2: Digital Sound

ABOUT THE UNIT

This unit involves pupils and students in the capture and manipulation of sounds using a variety of methods and devices. This includes sounds that they make themselves as well as sounds that others make.

This unit is divided into 4 sub-units:

1. Introduction to sound-making instruments

2. Recording sounds produced by pupils and instant playback

3. Producing sounds other than those made by action on object

4. Altering sounds using digital equipment.

WHERE THE UNIT FITS IN	TECHNICAL VOCABULARY	RESOURCES
This unit allows children with special educational needs to access curriculum learning opportunities/experiences, not typically available within a school context, via the use of ICT. The scheme covers the ICT POS with regard to using switches to operate a range of computer hardware and capturing, storing and retrieving digital images. This unit assumes that: • staff have access to technical equipment – typical of that found in a City Learning Centre • staff have access to relevant software and expertise • learning objectives for ICT and for other areas (e.g. motor/sensory skills) are included.	• Sample • Microphone • Computer • Keyboard • .wav file • Sound changer • Sythesiser • Sound • Loud/quiet • High/low (sounds) • Feedback	• Range of instruments • Digital sound maker • Sound-player software • Sampling software • .wav editor • Microphones • Sound recording software • Digital still camera • Digital video camera

EXPECTATIONS LINKED TO P LEVELS	
TOLERATE *(Encounter)*	Pupils are willing to be present during an experience or activity. For some pupils who may typically withhold their attention or presence from many situations, their willingness to tolerate, e.g. making sounds, may in itself be significant
REACT *(Awareness)*	Pupils react to sounds by changing their pattern of behaviour, e.g. briefly react to an instrument or recorded sound
RESPOND *(Attention and response)*	Pupils change their body language, e.g. facial expression, as a result of a stimulus such as a sound. Pupils may show delight, surprise or dissatisfaction as a response to the activity.
ENGAGE *(Engagement)*	Pupils make a more purposeful movement or show more consistent attention to events during the activity. They may watch an instrument being played, or may listen to sounds as they are digitally altered.
ANTICIPATE *(participation)*	Pupils positively or negatively anticipate outcomes such as the hitting of a drum. They may show signs of excitement in their willingness to participate in the activity; for example, wanting to take a turn using an instrument. They may be reluctant to take part – indicating an understanding of what is likely to happen. Some staff encouragement may be involved.
CHOOSE *(involvement)*	Pupils choose to be involved in the activity or make choices during the activity. They may request stimulus, e.g. by pointing or looking at an instrument in order to communicate a desire to be involved.
LINK EXPERIENCES *(gaining skills and understanding)*	Pupils make use of skills, knowledge, concepts or understanding from previous learning experiences. They recognise instruments and sounds. They may know that a drumstick is used to beat a drum.
Progression within Linking Experiences (moving from concrete through to more abstract application)	
P4 (concrete, repetition)	Pupils intentionally make or change a sound.
P5 (link to model)	Pupils use the icons in a sound program to select specific sounds.
P6 (understand how to make changes)	Pupils use a sound changer to deliberately change the sound, indicating an understanding of the effect of changing the position of their hand.
P7 (apply to range of new situations)	Pupils choose a preferred sound from a selection played to them.
P8 (apply sequentially with understanding)	Pupils demonstrate the use of sound in the final presentation to an audience.

LEARNING OBJECTIVES	POSSIBLE TEACHING ACTIVITIES	LEARNING / EXPERIENCES	POINTS TO NOTE
PUPILS SHOULD LEARN / EXPERIENCE			

SUB-UNIT 1: INTRODUCTION TO SOUND-MAKING INSTRUMENTS
Setting the scene

The first session will last approximately two hours, or possibly more if there are a larger number of children in the group.

It is important that:

- all pupils are positioned appropriately to ensure that they are aware of the device being used, and are involved in the activity
- individual pupils are positioned appropriately relative to the access device or instrument when it is their opportunity to produce sounds.

LEARNING OBJECTIVES	POSSIBLE TEACHING ACTIVITIES	LEARNING / EXPERIENCES	POINTS TO NOTE
• how to change or produce sounds using body movement • to use gross motor skills and develop coordination • to use auditory discrimination	• Use a sound changer to make sounds • Change the sounds produced by moving a limb or head across the device's detector • Compare the effect of moving body parts towards and away from the device	• The unit can make different sounds • The unit makes a different sound as a limb is moved closer to/further away from the unit • Choose a sound for inclusion in the presentation in Unit 3	• Different sounds result from localised movement • Deliberate use of body parts to produce desired sound • Recognition of changes (e.g. pitch, volume distortion) of sound	• Movements to change sound should be either voluntary or prompted on the part of the pupil. In the case of pupils tolerating an experience the movement would be directed by a familiar adult.

LEARNING OBJECTIVES	POSSIBLE TEACHING ACTIVITIES	LEARNING / EXPERIENCES	POINTS TO NOTE
PUPILS SHOULD LEARN / EXPERIENCE			

SUB-UNIT 2: RECORDING SOUNDS MADE BY PUPILS AND INSTANT PLAYBACK
Setting the scene

In this block, the pupils focus on one instrument at a time. Their reactions to the activity are videoed.

It is important that:

- only one instrument is played during each session to allow pupils to become familiar with the sounds produced
- individual pupils are positioned appropriately relative to the access device or instrument when it is their opportunity to produce sounds.

LEARNING OBJECTIVES	POSSIBLE TEACHING ACTIVITIES	LEARNING / EXPERIENCES	POINTS TO NOTE
- to use a range of body movements to produce a range of sounds using different instruments - to use gross motor skills and develop co-ordination - to use auditory discrimination	- Using a range of instruments pupils will make a range of sounds (e.g. keyboard, synthesiser, drum kit, voice etc.)	- Electronic instruments make a range of sounds - Match electronic instrument or image to a sound - Choose an instrument for later inclusion in Unit 3.	- Other instruments make a variety of sounds - Deliberate use of a body part to produce a range of sounds - Recognise that sounds are varied	- Movements to change sound should be either voluntary or prompted on the part of the pupil. In the case of pupils tolerating an experience the movement would be directed by a familiar adult. - **Unit 3: Communication** will result in a library CD-ROM which can be used to support follow-up activity involving matching sounds to instruments.

LEARNING OBJECTIVES	POSSIBLE TEACHING ACTIVITIES	LEARNING / EXPERIENCES	POINTS TO NOTE
PUPILS SHOULD LEARN / EXPERIENCE			

SUB-UNIT 3: PRODUCING SOUNDS OTHER THAN THOSE MADE BY ACTION ON OBJECT
Setting the scene

In this block, the pupils will focus on one sound source at a time.

It is important that:

- only one instrument is played during each session to allow pupils to become familiar with the sounds produced
- individual pupils are positioned appropriately relative to the access device or instrument when it is their opportunity to produce sounds
- recorded sounds are played back immediately.

LEARNING OBJECTIVES	POSSIBLE TEACHING ACTIVITIES	LEARNING / EXPERIENCES	POINTS TO NOTE
• to produce sounds in a variety of ways • to record and save sounds on a computer • to play back sounds on a computer • to use auditory discrimination	• Pupils produce a variety of sounds • Pupils record sounds using a switch, other access device, keyboard or mouse • Pupils play back sounds using a switch, other access device, keyboard or mouse	• that sounds can be produced in a variety of ways • that sounds can be recorded and saved using a computer • that sounds can be played back using a computer	• indicate a preference for particular sounds • controlled use of fine motor skills to produce a range of sounds	• Movements to change sound should be either voluntary or prompted on the part of the pupil. In the case of pupils tolerating an experience the movement would be directed by a familiar adult. • **Unit 3: Communication** will result in a library CD-ROM which can be used to support follow-up activity involving listening to, and expressing preferences for, pre-recorded sounds

LEARNING OBJECTIVES	POSSIBLE TEACHING ACTIVITIES	LEARNING / EXPERIENCES	POINTS TO NOTE
PUPILS SHOULD LEARN / EXPERIENCE			
SUB-UNIT 4: ALTERING SOUNDS USING DIGITAL EQUIPMENT **Setting the scene** In this block, the pupils will focus on one sound source at a time. It is important that: • only one instrument is played during each session to allow pupils to become familiar with the sounds produced • individual pupils are positioned appropriately relative to the access device or instrument when it is their opportunity to produce sounds • recorded sounds are played back immediately.			
• to use fine motor skills • to explore a single sound which has had its pitch altered • to explore a single sound which has been altered in other ways (e.g. reverb, distortion, parametric eq., reverse etc.) • to use auditory discrimination	• Pupils access a pre-recorded sample of a familiar sound, and use a midi input device to play it back at different pitches (using sampling software) • Pupils are presented with a set of sound files which have been created from the single sample used in the activity above, which has been altered in several ways. These are played back using appropriate software and access devices (e.g. Clicker and switches)	• recognise that a sound can be altered by a range of devices (e.g. effects unit, .wav editor) • controlled use of fine motor skills to produce a range of altered sounds • recognise that sounds have been altered • indicate a preference for particular altered sounds	• Movements to access altered sounds should be either voluntary or prompted on the part of the pupil. In the case of pupils tolerating an experience the movement would be directed by a familiar adult. • **Unit 3: Communication** will result in a library CD-ROM which can be used to support follow-up activity involving listening to, and expressing preferences for, pre-recorded sounds

Unit 3: Communication

ICT SEN
KS4

ABOUT THE UNIT

This unit involves pupils and students in the presentation of the work they have carried out so far, to a selected audience of staff, peers, and parents/carers.

This unit is divided into 3 sub-units:

1. Selecting content for the final presentation

2. Watching the final presentation

3. Giving the final presentation to an audience.

WHERE THE UNIT FITS IN

This unit allows children with special educational needs to access curriculum learning opportunities/experiences, not typically available within a school context, via the use of ICT. The scheme covers the ICT POS with regard to using switches to operate a range of computer hardware and capturing, storing and retrieving digital images and sounds.

This unit assumes that:

- staff have access to technical equipment – typical of that found in a City Learning Centre
- staff have access to relevant software and expertise
- learning objectives for ICT and for other areas (e.g. motor/sensory skills) are included.

TECHNICAL VOCABULARY

- Image
- Camera
- Digital video
- Projector
- Screen
- Computer
- Printer
- Floppy disk
- Memory card
- Tripod
- Capture
- Save
- Load

RESOURCES

- Digital still camera
- Digital video camera
- Digital video cassettes
- Video-editing software
- Batteries
- Data projector
- Screen
- Floppy disk
- Tripod
- Switches

EXPECTATIONS LINKED TO P LEVELS	
TOLERATE (Encounter)	Pupils are willing to be present during an experience or activity. For some pupils who may typically withhold their attention or presence from many situations, their willingness to tolerate, e.g. being the focus of attention of an audience, may in itself be significant.
REACT (Awareness)	Pupils react to audience responses by changing their pattern of behaviour, e.g. briefly react to a round of applause.
RESPOND (Attention and response)	Pupils change their body language, e.g. facial expression, as a result of a stimulus such as an audience response (laughter, applause, etc.). Pupils may show delight, surprise or dissatisfaction as a response to the activity.
ENGAGE (Engagement)	Pupils make a more purposeful movement or show more consistent attention to events during the activity. They may watch audience reaction to their presentation, or purposefully activate a switch to advance their presentation.
ANTICIPATE (participation)	Pupils positively or negatively anticipate outcomes such as an image of themselves on a screen. They may show signs of excitement in their willingness to participate in the activity; for example, demonstrate something to an audience. They may be reluctant to take part – indicating an understanding of what is likely to happen. Some staff encouragement may be involved.
CHOOSE (involvement)	Pupils choose to be involved in the activity or make choices during the activity. They may request stimulus, e.g. by pointing or looking at a still image to be included in their presentation.
LINK EXPERIENCES (gaining skills and understanding)	Pupils make use of skills, knowledge, concepts or understanding from previous learning experiences. They recognise familiar images or equipment. They may know that a button needs to be pressed to capture an image.
Progression within Linking Experiences (moving from concrete through to more abstract application)	
P4 (concrete, repetition)	Pupils follow step-by-step instructions to carry out a basic process, e.g. they will purposefull use a camera to capture an image.
P5 (link to model)	Pupils follow instructions involving more than one step at a time; for example, they capture an image using a digital camera following instructions. Pupils indicate changes such as when watching recorded footage of themselves they realise they are wearing different clothing.
P6 (understand how to make changes)	Pupils observe changes within the video and make a connection between the image and themselves, e.g. pupils move their hands and feet to ensure they appear on the projected image on the screen.
P7 (apply to range of new situations)	Pupils look through a series of images and select a favourite one, e.g. to save or print.
P8 (apply sequentially with understanding)	Pupils know that images are stored and can be retrieved for a floppy disk. They respond to new terminology and can find objects when asked, e.g. will put a finger on the button or operate the printer when asked.

LEARNING OBJECTIVES	POSSIBLE TEACHING ACTIVITIES	LEARNING / EXPERIENCES	POINTS TO NOTE
PUPILS SHOULD LEARN / EXPERIENCE			
SUB-UNIT 1: SELECTING CONTENT FOR FINAL PRESENTATION **Setting the scene** The first session will involve pupils in selecting their favourite video clip, still images and sounds from those which they saved in Units 1 and 2. It is important that: • all pupils are positioned appropriately to ensure that they have a good view of the projected image or video, and can hear recorded sounds sufficiently • all pupils have the opportunity to respond • a computer is used to play back all media			
• that sounds, moving and still images can be stored and retrieved using a computer • to respond to recorded media of themselves, and their peers • to express a preference for particular sounds, videos and still images	• Using a computer to project stored video on a large screen • Using a computer to project stored still images on a large screen • Using a computer to play back sounds on amplified speakers		• Reactions indicating a positive or negative response to images must be voluntary or prompted on the part of the pupil. A familiar adult may need to interpret these responses in the case of some pupils

LEARNING OBJECTIVES	POSSIBLE TEACHING ACTIVITIES	LEARNING / EXPERIENCES	POINTS TO NOTE
PUPILS SHOULD LEARN / EXPERIENCE			

SUB-UNIT 2: WATCHING THE FINAL PRESENTATION
Setting the scene

In this block, the pupils watch the final presentation slideshow of the media which they previously selected. This slideshow has been prepared by the project team for each pupil.

It is important that:

- each pupil's presentation is displayed in turn, and all pupils watch each other's presentation
- pupils are positioned appropriately so that they all have a good view of the screen
- the pupils can see that the presentation slides are being advanced by pressing a large switch
- pupils get the opportunity to attempt to advance the presentations using the switch.

LEARNING OBJECTIVES	POSSIBLE TEACHING ACTIVITIES	LEARNING / EXPERIENCES	POINTS TO NOTE
• that stored images, video and sounds can be displayed in different ways (i.e. in a complete presentation package) • that the slides in a presentation can be advanced manually	• Pupils start off by viewing each presentation in turn, as an audience • Pupils have the opportunity to advance the presentation themselves as the presenter	• that a camera can store still images • that stored images can be reviewed later • that images can be projected onto a large screen • that stored sounds can be replayed later	• controlled use of gross and fine motor skills to advance slides at appropriate times
			• Movements to advance the presentation should be either voluntary or prompted on the part of the pupil. In the case of pupils tolerating an experience the movement would be directed by a familiar adult. • **Unit 3: Communication** will result in an interactive CD-ROM which can be used to support follow-up activity involving matching movement to recorded footage.

LEARNING OBJECTIVES	POSSIBLE TEACHING ACTIVITIES	LEARNING / EXPERIENCES	POINTS TO NOTE
PUPILS SHOULD LEARN / EXPERIENCE			

SUB-UNIT 3: FINAL PRESENTATION
Setting the scene

In this block, the pupils present the work in which they have been involved to an invited audience.

It is important that:

• the pupils act as the presenter, positioned in front of the audience and to the side of a projection screen. They advance the slides in the presentation, with assistance when necessary.

LEARNING OBJECTIVES	POSSIBLE TEACHING ACTIVITIES	LEARNING / EXPERIENCES	POINTS TO NOTE
• that stored images, video and sounds can be displayed in different ways (i.e. in a complete presentation package). • that the slides in a presentation can be advanced manually	• pupils use a big switch to advance through the slides in the presentation	• that a camera can store still images • that stored images can be reviewed later • that images can be projected onto a large screen • that stored sounds can be replayed later • to respond to the reactions of the audience to the presentation	• Movements to advance the presentation should be either voluntary or prompted on the part of the pupil. In the case of pupils tolerating on experience the movement would be directed by a familiar adult.

111

References

Barton, L. (2001) *Disability, Politics and the Struggle for Change*. London: David Fulton.

CSIE (2002) *Index for Inclusion*.

DFE (1994) *Careers Education and Special Educational Needs*. DFE Circular 6/94.

DfES (1997a) *Excellence in Schools*.

DfES (1997b) *Excellence for All Children: Meeting Special Educational Needs*.

DfES (1998) *Meeting Special Educational Needs: A Programme of Action*.

DfES (2000) National Curriculum.

DfES (2001) *Inclusive Schooling: Children with Special Educational Needs*.

DfES (2001a) SEN Revised Code of Practice.

DfES (2003) Report of the Special School Working Party. London: DfES.

DfES/QCA (1999a) *The National Curriculum: Key Stages 3 and 4*. Department for Education and Skills and Qualifications and Curriculum Authority.

DfES/QCA (1999b) *The National Curriculum: Key Stages 1 and 2*. Department for Education and Skills and Qualifications and Curriculum Authority.

Disability Rights Task Force (1999) *From Exclusion to Inclusion*.

Dyson, A. (2001) 'Special needs in the 21st century: where are we going?' *British Journal of Special Education*, 28(1), March.

Education Leeds (2000) Inclusion of Pupils with SEN Policy.

Jupp, K. (1992) *Everyone Belongs*. London: Souvenir Press.

Norwich, B. (2002) *LEA Inclusion Trends in England 1997–2001*. Bristol: CSIE.

QCA (1996) KS1 and 2 Schemes of Work for ICT.

QCA (1998) *Schemes of Work for Key Stages 1 and 2*. Qualifications and Curriculum Authority.

QCA (2000a) *Updates to Schemes of Work for Key Stages 1 and 2*. Qualifications and Curriculum Authority.

QCA (2000b) *Schemes of Work for Key Stage 3*. Qualifications and Curriculum Authority.

QCA (2000c) *A Scheme of Work for Key Stage 3: ICT*. London: QCA Publications.

QCA (2001) *Planning, Teaching and Assessing the Curriculum for Pupils with Learning Difficulties: ICT*. London: QCA Publications.

QCA (2001a) *Planning, Teaching and Assessing the Curriculum for Pupils with Learning Difficulties: Personal, Social and Health Education and Citizenship*.

SCAA (1996) *Planning the Curriculum for Pupils with Profound and Multiple Learning Difficulties*. School Curriculum and Assessment Council and Curriculum and Assessment Authority for Wales.

Singleton (2002) 'TRREACLE: a practical approach to planning for and assessing the progress of pupils with learning difficulties'. *School Science Review*, **83** (305), June, 41–50.

Thomas *et al.* (1997) *British Journal of Special Education*, 25(1).

Index

UNIVERSITY OF WALES, NEWPORT LIBRARY AND INFORMATION SERVICES CAERLEON